WELCOME

scrapbooking has always been a hands-on affair, with hours of thoughtful cutting, pasting, cropping, and arranging. But as computers have become part of our everyday lives, they too, have influenced our scrapbooking. Although some scrapbookers start simply, with an easy computer-generated title or journaling block to complement their traditional handmade layouts, others delve into their scrapbooking with nothing more than a blank computer screen, a blinking cursor, and a downloaded photo ripe for a red-eye fix and special effects.

Whatever your digital skill level, *Point-and-Click Scrapbooking* can help you get started, with valuable information and techniques on everything from taking and improving your photos to creating your own fantastic photo effects. We'll help you decipher digital jargon and inspire you with remarkable digital layouts. We'll even share online resources to help make your digital scrapbooking easier.

So sit back, browse through our pages, and discover all the rewards of scrapbooking in the digital age.

HAPPY SCRAPBOOKING!

TABLE OF CONTENTS

2

15

52

82

THE PHOTOS AND LAYERED-TEXT MAT on this page were printed out on Anita Matejka's computer printer, as was the journaling that frames the page. To simulate the look of parade floats attached to long strings, Anita used vellum tags strung to her photo mat to create this page. Using a square punch that was smaller than the tag, she punched a hole in each tag and then adhered photos to the back of each one.

SOURCES: COMPUTER FONT IS VEGETABLE SOUP BY TWO PEAS IN A BUCKET. TAGS AND EYELETS BY MAKING MEMORIES. RUB-ONS BY CREATIVE IMAGINATIONS. COMPUTER SOFTWARE IS PHOTOIMPACT 8.0 BY ULEAD. **DESIGN BY ANITA MATEJKA.**

MARGIE LUNDY CREATED this layout about the adoptions of her son and her friend's daughter. The key to making this layout appear to have been assembled by hand instead of on a computer was adding drop shadows to several elements. She added shadows to help the letters in the title stand out from the background. Margie also added drop shadows to the photo mats as well as her journaling block. The flower eyelets were copied from the flowers in the photos, which Margie then beveled, contoured, and finished with a drop shadow to add dimension and create the look of real eyelets.

SOURCES: COMPUTER FONTS ARE CURLZ ("CHILDREN") BY AGFA-MONOTYPE, FORMAL SCRIPT ("COME FROM") DOWNLOADED OFF THE INTERNET, ALGERIAN ("GOD") BY ELSNER+FLAKE, BLACKADDER ("FOR SOME") BY ITC, JANIE ("THE JOURNEY") BY HALLMARK, CRICKET ("HOME") BY ARTTODAY, CHARADE ("JUST TAKES") BY JUKEBOX, BORDEAUX LIGHT ("A LITTLE") BY ARTTODAY, SCRAP HAP'NEN ("LONGER") BY INSPIRE GRAPHICS, ARIZONA ("ALL") BY TWO PEAS IN A BUCKET, AND DONNY'S HAND (JOURNALING), ALL DOWNLOADED OFF THE INTERNET. COMPUTER SOFTWARE IS ADOBE PHOTOSHOP. **DESIGN BY MARGIE LUNDY.**

WHETHER YOU USE YOUR COMPUTER TO CREATE INDIVIDUAL ACCENTS OR ENTIRE SCRAPBOOK PAGES, YOU'LL LOVE THE CREATIVE FREEDOM THAT GOING DIGITAL AFFORDS.

ARTICLE BY ANITA MATEJKA

GOING [DIGITAL]

SINCE THE MOMENT MY FINGERTIPS FIRST MADE CONTACT WITH A COMPUTER KEYBOARD, I'VE BEEN HOOKED. THERE WAS NO GOING BACK FOR ME. I HAD DISCOVERED A WAY TO DO THINGS MORE EFFICIENTLY AND MORE GRAPHICALLY PLEASING THAN EVER BEFORE, AND IT FOREVER CHANGED THE WAY I GO ABOUT MANY OF MY TASKS—EVEN SCRAPBOOKING.

Whether it's something as basic as creating a title or a journaling block or a bit more elaborate like digitally tinting a photo or making a full-blown page, I've incorporated the power of the computer into my scrapbook world, and I want you to know how easy it is for you to do the same. Although we can't possibly touch on every possible feature of digital design, we will cover quite a few fun techniques that I hope will inspire you to experiment on your own!

Before jumping into the driver's seat, remember a couple of important items: When working with a digital photo or layout, create a backup copy of your work. Use the Save As option to ensure that you don't save over the original photo or artwork. (I've learned this the hard way!)

To get the best printing results, always save images in your program's native format or in TIFF, PNG, or JPG format (uncompressed). When you save in the program's native format, you'll maintain all layers and settings. Although you'll end up with slightly larger file sizes than in some other formats, this option is the most reliable.

Most importantly, take the time to familiarize yourself with your digital-imaging program. Go through all the menu bars, filters, and effects to see what you can and can't do. Check out the "KEY" boxes throughout this article. They'll provide you with vital information that will help ensure your computer scrapbooking experience is the best it can be. Now, buckle up and enjoy the ride as we take a trip down digital lane!

GET YOUR MOTOR RUNNING

If you want to ease into the computer-generated scrapbook world without feeling overwhelmed, start with a few basic techniques that will enhance your traditional scrapbook pages with little effort. Word-processing programs such as Microsoft Word can handle most of the text-generated techniques. For photo editing and printing, check out the basic digital-imaging programs in the "KEY: Software" box on page 4.

Note: *When working in Word, make sure your Drawing toolbar is visible. You usually can find it at the bottom of your screen. If not, go to View, then Toolbars, and select Drawing.*

CUSTOM LETTER TEMPLATES

If you like the look of lettering templates but can't find the perfect size or style, reverse-text printing with your computer is a great alternative. You can use any font, and it's very easy to do.

Open Word and look for the blue tilted "A" on the Drawing toolbar. After clicking on "A," select the top left square that shows an outlined version of WordArt. Click on OK, and move on to the next step.

EACH AUTUMN, AS THE LEAVES OF HER FRONT-YARD SUGAR
maple change hue, Christina White revels in the rich, blazing color.
Watching from her front window, she marks the seasons by the
tree's foliage, and on the day this photo was taken, the brilliant red
leaves and the crisp blue sky made for a stunning combination.
(Christina notes that although this photo was taken digitally, the
colors were not digitally enhanced.) To construct her computer-
generated layout, Christina first used the eyedropper tool in her
software to collect a red color from the leaves to use for the
background. Utilizing layers, opacity, feathering, and the stroke tool,
she created the white lines and highlights used in each background
rectangle. A final layer included individual letter blocks as well as
whimsical word art for her title.

SOURCES: COMPUTER FONT IS ZAPF ELLIPTICAL BY BITSTREAM. PHOTO-EDITING
SOFTWARE IS ADOBE PHOTOSHOP ELEMENTS 2. **DESIGN BY CHRISTINA WHITE.**

KEY: Software

Selecting a software program for your digital-imaging needs is
sort of like shopping for a car. There are basic models that will
get you to and from work, there are intermediate models with a
few extras that make summer vacations easier, and then there
are the cars that have every bell and whistle imaginable and can
take you around the world and back. Digital-imaging programs
are much the same.

Basic programs that will do simple photo and text editing start
at approximately $30 to $50 (Ulead Photo Express My
Scrapbook 2 and Microsoft Picture It! Premium). Intermediate
programs run anywhere from $90 to $100 (JASC Paintshop Pro,
Ulead PhotoImpact, and Adobe Photoshop Elements). An
advanced program like Adobe Photoshop can cost $600 to
$700. That's quite a difference in price, and it's important to
think about what options are important to you before you drive it
home. For most people (myself included), programs in the $100
and under range are sufficient for most digital-imaging needs.
However, Photoshop is a very powerful program, and if you plan
on becoming a professional photographer or designer, you'll
probably want to consider it. Also, before you rush out to buy
new software, check the CDs that came with your printer,
scanner, or digital camera. Often, programs are bundled
with your peripherals.

It's hard to determine which program is right for you
without a test-drive, which is why many companies offer a
free 30-day-trial download feature on their Web sites.
Check the chart at right for more information.

Type in your title and select the font you would like to use.
(Unfortunately, you can see only font names and not what different
fonts look like in this menu, so choose a font before going into
WordArt.) Click OK, and it will add your new title to your document.
Grab the little squares on the corners and sides to resize the title to
the dimensions you want. Then select Flip Horizontal from the Draw
drop-down menu in the bottom left corner of your screen.

Print out your title on the back of your paper, and then cut it out
and attach it to your page.

JOURNALING THAT SPANS A 12" PAGE

Just because you don't have a 12" printer doesn't mean you can't print
journaling the width of your page. Adjust your Page Setup by
changing the Orientation to Landscape, modifying the Width to 12"
wide, and making the Height no taller than 8½". Make the Height
number smaller for a shorter journaling block—I usually make mine
about 4" tall and drag my top margin down a couple of inches. Run a
test print on scratch paper before printing the final version.

Program	Trial Available Online	Level	Retail Price	Web Site
Ulead PhotoImpact 10.1	30 days	Intermediate-Advanced	$90	www.ulead.com
Ulead Photo Express My Scrapbook 2	N/A	Basic	$30	www.ulead.com
Microsoft Picture It! Premium	Demo available	Intermediate-Advanced	$50	www.microsoft.com/products/imaging
Microsoft Digital Image Pro!	Demo available	Basic	$90	www.microsoft.com/products/imaging
JASC Paintshop Pro	30 days	Intermediate-Advanced	$95	www.jasc.com
Adobe Photoshop CS	Tryout version	Advanced	$650	www.adobe.com
Adobe Photoshop Elements	Tryout version	Intermediate	$90	www.adobe.com

THIS ENTIRE LAYOUT WAS DESIGNED AND PRODUCED DIGITALLY. First, Anita layered digital paper on a solid black background, darkening the red to better match her photo. To make the eyelets, she created a circle shape and changed it to 3D Pipe, which hollows out the center while adding shading. She added an additional shadow to each to make them more realistic. The downloaded digital fibers were changed to black to coordinate with the page, and digital clip art was used to dress up the design. Anita typed her journaling over the photo in white, taking care not to cover the subjects.

SOURCES: DIGITAL PAPER AND CLIP ART BY PCCRAFTER. COMPUTER FONTS ARE BLACK JACK (ON PHOTO) BY TYPADELIC AND BIRDHOUSE (HEADLINE) DOWNLOADED OFF THE INTERNET. FAUX FIBERS DESIGNED BY SHANNON AT SCRAPBOOK-BYTES.COM. COMPUTER SOFTWARE IS PHOTOIMPACT 8.0 BY ULEAD. **DESIGN BY ANITA MATEJKA.**

When printing black-and-white photos, adjust your print options by selecting black ink instead of color and you'll avoid getting purple or blue printouts. If you're working with scanned photos, be sure to check out the "KEY: Scanning" box, below, before proceeding.

CONVERTING TO BLACK-AND-WHITE

One common technique when working with digital images is turning color prints into black-and-white. Some digital-imaging programs have made the process as easy as clicking a button. If the program you're using doesn't have a "magic" button, look in the Format, Effect, or Image menu. For instance, in Photoshop, go to Image and then Mode, and select Grayscale to change your image to a gray-scale version.

ADDING TEXT TO PHOTOS

Creating a caption, writing a title, or adding journaling to your photos before printing them is a breeze. Open a copy of your digital image in your photo-editing program. Click on the "T" or Text Tool, and select the font, color, and size of type you want to use. Click anywhere on your photo and begin typing. If you want to move the text or delete it, click on your selection tool (usually an arrow), select the text, and move it to the appropriate location. Then all you need to do is hit Save As and Print.

KEY: Scanning

Dpi, ppi … it's all so confusing! These are some of the terms you'll need to understand if you're going to find success as a digital scrapbooker. "Dpi" stands for "dots per inch," and "ppi" stands for "pixels per inch." Our monitor reads images in pixels, while our printer reads them in dots. If you're working with a scanner and want quality printouts, understanding dpi (or actually ppi) and how to get the best results is crucial.

A dpi number tells your printer how far apart to space the dots in a 1-inch area. If you print an image at 75 dpi, the dots will be spaced farther apart than if you were to print the image at 300 dpi. At 300 dpi, the closer dots would create a crisper image. Ppi works the same, but it deals more with the image appearance on the screen. Dpi is what controls the printer output, so the higher the dpi, the better the quality.

It's hard to get much higher than 300 ppi from a scanned image. But if you plan to enlarge your image, then you must scan at a higher resolution or it will become pixilated once you resize to the larger image format. If you plan on enlarging, follow these guidelines:

Resolution dpi = (pixels of length) ÷ (inches of length). If you have an image that is 1,200 pixels of length (your scanner should give you this information after it does a preliminary scan of the image) and you want it to be 10" long, you would have a resolution of 120 dpi, which would not produce a quality image. If you wanted to have a resolution of 300, divide 1,200 by 300 and you would come up with 4" in length. Therefore, if you want a higher resolution scan with a larger image, you need to increase your image size *before* you scan.

Most scanners allow you to increase the image size by a certain percentage before scanning. If you think you'll be printing your photo at a larger size than the original, make these changes before you scan the image, and also scan at 600 dpi to be safe.

In general, if you want a larger print size, then you'll need to use either a lower printed resolution or a larger scanned image (scan at 150 percent or 200 percent). If you want increased resolution, you need either a larger image or a smaller printed size.

THIS LAYOUT IS A MIX of traditional and computer scrapbooking techniques. Anita downloaded a clip art series off the Internet and printed a tag and two accent pieces onto matte photo paper. Matte paper creates a more realistic look because it lacks the super-shiny gloss of other photo papers. She mounted the accents on vellum and added fibers to the top of the tag.

SOURCES: PATTERNED PAPERS BY PROVO CRAFT. COMPUTER FONT IS ROCK STAR BY TWO PEAS IN A BUCKET. CLIP ART BY PCCRAFTER. PHOTO PAPER BY EPSON. RIVETS BY CHATTERBOX. FIBERS BY RUBBA DUB DUB. COMPUTER SOFTWARE IS PHOTOIMPACT 8.0 BY ULEAD. **DESIGN BY ANITA MATEJKA.**

CUSTOMIZED CLIP ART

The market today is full of wonderful clip art sources. One of my favorite places to visit is www.pccrafter.com. This site has a great selection of Creatables designed by a variety of artists, each with their own style. Easy-to-use packages can be downloaded for about $5 each. The graphics come in different formats for different needs—black-and-white (WMF format), color (WMF format), and painted (JPG format). The color images are easy to alter in Microsoft Word or your imaging program.

Microsoft also has an online service called Design Gallery Live (http://dgl.microsoft.com) that has thousands of images (clip art, photos, sounds, etc.) available for download. If neither of those sites has what you're looking for, do a search online for free clip art.

It's easy and fun to customize WMF (Windows Metafile) graphics. If you're using Word, you can import other WMF files (such as Creatables) into the Clip Art Gallery and have them all at your fingertips. Just go to your menu bar and select Insert, Picture, and Clip Art to open the Clip Art Gallery. From there, select Import Clips at the top of the dialog box. You'll then need to locate the WMF files in the directory in which they're stored. Once you've imported these graphics into your Clip Art Gallery, you can double-click on the graphic to use it.

To alter image colors, click on the image and select Edit Picture from the drop-down menu. You'll be taken to a new box where you can click on different elements of the image and use the Paint Bucket on your Drawing toolbar to change the color. It's just that easy to get custom clip art!

HEAD OUT ON THE HIGHWAY

Once you're feeling comfortable with some of the techniques we've described, you're ready to move on to slightly more complicated approaches. Not all of them take special software. Use a word-processing program to rotate, layer, and color text for fun effects. Play with font sizes, styles, and colors to create custom photo mats or even background paper. Then try these more complicated image-editing techniques.

CLONING

Done right, cloning can work wonders when touching up photos. For instance, in the Star City Parade layout, *page 2*, I selected a photo of my children to use as the focal point, but there were some distracting items in the background. Using the clone brush in my image-editing program, I selected an area that I wanted to duplicate and started brushing away. Be sure to change the areas you sample often, so the blending looks realistic.

TINTED PHOTOS

Hand-tinting photos gives them a classic look, and today's image-editing programs make the task simpler than ever. Here are a few of the easiest methods:

● Create a duplicate of your image, and change the duplicate to black-and-white. As previously mentioned, some programs come with a quick-click button to perform this function; otherwise, look

to know is nothing at all;
to imagine is everything.

FOR THIS DIGITALLY DESIGNED LAYOUT, Wendi Speciale adjusted the saturation of the repeated detail shot— the back of the head photos— giving each a different color background. She used the same photo in its entirety to create the bulk of this two-page design, employing a simple technique to mimic the look of a hand-tinted image. She made a copy of the picture and pasted it on top of the original. She then converted the top layer to black-and-white and used the eraser tool to delete areas she wanted to be in color.

SOURCES: COMPUTER FONT IS HELDA SMASHED DOWNLOADED OFF THE INTERNET. COMPUTER SOFTWARE IS ADOBE PHOTOSHOP. DESIGN BY WENDI SPECIALE.

WHILE TRAVELING IN Luxembourg, Christine MacIlvaine and her family stopped at churches to light candles in memory of Christine's mother. Using photos from one stop, Christine created this layout with a soft glow that mimics the candlelight. She did this by using filters to give color only to the center of the photo, leaving the rest of the image black-and-white. For the background, Christine used a photo of stained-glass windows that she blurred and applied a transparency effect to soften the look.

SOURCES: COMPUTER FONTS ARE SCRIPTINA ("FAITH"), DOWNLOADED OFF THE INTERNET, AND GARAMOND ITALIC ("IS A CANDLE") BY ITC. COMPUTER SOFTWARE IS ADOBE PHOTOSHOP ELEMENTS AND MICROSOFT DIGITAL IMAGE PRO. DESIGN BY CHRISTINE MacILVAINE.

Faith

is a candle *aglow* in the night, showing the way with its *comforting* urging us *onward*, whatever's before us -- shining with promise to heal and *restore* us.

KEY: Output Options

You have several options for outputting your digital creations. The option you choose may affect the size you work in, so research your options carefully before you start.

INK-JET PRINTERS

Several printers on the market can print both text and photos well and start at approximately $100. When photo printers first came out, many questioned the longevity of the prints. However, companies are constantly improving the archival qualities of their printers, inks, and papers. Many of today's printer/paper/ink combinations result in prints that will last as long, if not longer, than traditional photographs under normal conditions.

When selecting a printer, research the total cost per page printed. Although you may be tempted to purchase a less expensive printer, you may end up paying more for ink cartridges or maintenance in the long run.

The printer isn't the only tool you must consider to get good printing results. Paper also plays a key role. Buy paper specifically made for photo printing when outputting photos or layouts. Most manufacturers also recommend using papers and ink cartridges made to work with the specific printer.

If you plan on printing out scrapbook pages that are 12×12", you'll need to research printers that can handle that size. Both Epson and Hewlett-Packard make excellent large-format printers. They cost a bit more but provide much more flexibility.

LAB SERVICES

Besides printing at home, you have several other options. Many photo labs can output images stored digitally, whether on a CD or a digital camera memory cartridge. Check with labs near you for the best price, compatible formats, and other services offered.

You also may want to try an online service such as www.snapfish.com, www.shutterfly.com, www.ofoto.com, or www.photoworks.com. (See page 45 for more information on online photo services.)

An additional benefit to having your images printed by a local or online lab is that they'll be printed on the same photo paper and with the same tools as traditional prints, which means that if you've digitally altered one image but the rest of the images you have on a layout are traditional prints, the two types will match much better.

[IF YOU NEED A **SMALLER FILE** FOR E-MAILING OR **STORAGE**, CONVERT YOUR IMAGE TO A **JPEG** AFTER YOU'RE COMPLETELY DONE AND HAVE **ALREADY SAVED** YOUR FILE IN THE PROGRAM'S FORMAT.]

---

under Hue & Saturation and move the Saturation slider all the way to -100. Another option is to change the Data Type to Grayscale. If this creates a new file, copy the whole image and paste it on top of the color image. This should create a new layer.

● Working on the black-and-white layer, use your eraser brush to erase the areas that you want to be tinted. The color portion of the image should begin to show through right away. If you make a mistake, stop and hit Undo. Save as you go.

● If you want to actually change the color of your image or tint the whole photo a different color, convert your image file to Grayscale and then change the Data Type again to RGB. You then can bring color back into the photo. Go to Edit, Fill, and select the color of your choice. Change the transparency to something like 80 percent and in the Merge field, select Hue & Saturation.

● To hand-color, select a brush and change the shape and size to work in the areas of your choice. When using this method, change the opacity (transparency) of your colors to somewhere between 15 and 40 percent so the photo still shows through.

RACE TO THE FINISH LINE

Are you ready for this? Throw your adhesive out the window, and make sure you're buckled in! Creating complete scrapbook pages on the computer can quickly become an addictive pastime, as many digital scrapbookers will attest. Designer Christine MacIlvaine told us, "I love the versatility and ease with which I can create terrific layouts. At the touch of a button, you can change fonts, line thickness, and color. The possibilities are endless!" She's definitely right about that! Being able to move objects around freely and getting colors to match perfectly are just a few of the benefits of scrapbooking digitally.

I've found that creating scrapbook pages on your computer takes a pretty tricked-out engine … I mean, computer. So, make sure you have sufficient memory to work on your pages. Before beginning any work, I suggest restarting your computer to refresh the memory and closing other programs to free up as much memory as possible. Also, save your work often to avoid any losses if your computer decides to take an unscheduled break!

As you begin to design digitally, you must first decide what your output options are. (See "KEY: Output Options," opposite.) Reach a decision before starting or risk wasting many hours designing in a size you can't output. Once you've settled on a size, open your digital-imaging program and select File and New. A dialog box will pop up asking you to input the size and resolution of your page. I usually set mine to between 240 and 300 dpi.

Just as there are many different layers on a traditional scrapbook page (paper, photo mats, photos, embellishments, etc.), it's important to understand the function of layers in your digital scrapbooking. Layers are a way to keep parts of your images separate from each other. (When working with your program's native format, the layers will be stored as is each time you save your file. However, if you save

as a JPG, the file will be flattened and you will no longer be able to make changes to individual pieces. Therefore, if you need a smaller file for e-mailing or storage, convert your image to a JPG after you're completely done and have already saved your file in the program's native format.)

Find the Layers palette in your program, and leave it open when working. If you want to move something down or up a layer but it's hard to grab with your cursor, use your Layers box to select the item. Just click the item you'll be moving in the Layers box and move it to the correct level. If you want your title to be on top of the photo instead of underneath it, make sure to drag the title above the photo in the Layers box. The more you utilize the Layers palette, the more you'll realize how helpful it is in moving and editing your layers.

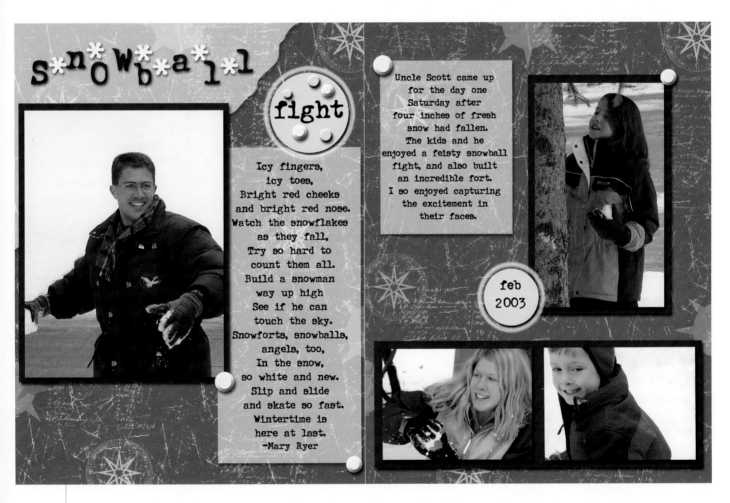

MICHELLE SHEFVELAND started this layout by making two 8.5×11" files with a coordinating background color. She mimicked the look of hand-stamped collage paper by using brushes in various sizes to create patterns. She used the color-chooser tool (the eyedropper) to match the color of one winter coat to the photo mats and to match the color of the snow for her journaling blocks. For a realistic vellum look, she reduced the opacity of the blocks to 55 percent. Drop shadows and beveled edges help give the "snowballs" and journaling a three-dimensional look.

SOURCES: COMPUTER FONT IS TYPEWRITER DOWNLOADED OFF THE INTERNET. COMPUTER SOFTWARE IS ADOBE PHOTOSHOP ELEMENTS 1.0.
DESIGN BY MICHELLE SHEFVELAND.

ANITA DESIGNED THIS PAGE entirely on her computer. She started with a white background and then layered a photo of the crowd on top. To soften the photo, she changed the opacity to 60 percent. A framed white box at 50 percent opacity is the ideal backdrop for her journaling. Anita then added her photos and used premade borders to outline each one. She also added shadows to the text and some elements to give them the illusion of depth.

SOURCES: COMPUTER FONTS ARE ROUGHBRUSH ("SEA"), AVALON (JOURNALING), AND VARSITY ("RED"), ALL DOWNLOADED OFF THE INTERNET. COMPUTER SOFTWARE IS PHOTOIMPACT 8.0 BY ULEAD. **DESIGN BY ANITA MATEJKA.**

FOR THE BACKGROUND of this computer-generated layout, Anita used a downloaded digital background paper and an enlarged photograph of her family's Thanksgiving tablecloth. By making the orange "paper" slightly transparent and using layers, she was able to make it look like the filmstrip was lying behind it. Anita rotated the filmstrip templates first and then resized and rotated her photos to fit the openings. To alter the colors in the photos, she used a duotone effect to select the amount of color that she wanted to show. To make the clear pebbles for the title, she altered a plain circle by editing its color and lighting to create the look she wanted.

SOURCES: DIGITAL PAPER BY PCCRAFTER. FILMSTRIP TEMPLATE BY DENIS GERMAIN FOR ESCRAPPERS.COM. COMPUTER FONT IS TYPEWRITER DOWNLOADED OFF THE INTERNET. COMPUTER SOFTWARE IS PHOTOIMPACT 8.0 BY ULEAD. **DESIGN BY ANITA MATEJKA.**

[ADDING **SHADOWS** TO YOUR TEXT, PHOTOS, TAGS, AND OTHER EMBELLISHMENTS IS A **GREAT WAY** TO CREATE A **REALISTIC** THREE-DIMENSIONAL EFFECT. **]**

KEY: Resources

A number of great online resources can help with your digital designing. If you're in the market for a printer or other computer supplies, check Web sites such as www.cnet.com, www.zdnet.com, or www.pcworld.com for side-by-side comparison shopping and consumer reviews. For great advice on scanning, check www.scantips.com.

Monitor calibration is important in achieving a printout that matches what's on your monitor. Most of the time that's the biggest frustration in printing, but by calibrating your monitor, you can avoid some printing headaches. Check www .epaper press.com/monitorcal/index/html or www .werbefoto.at/d_base/calibration.htm for more information.

I've also found a number of great tutorials online during my research. For general advice and guidance on computer scrapbooking, see http://myjanee.home.insightbb.com and www.scrapbook-bytes.com.

MAKING FAUX EMBELLISHMENTS

You can make some amazing faux embellishments with just a little time and effort. For instance, to create a tag, use the Shape Path tool to create the size and shape you want. Once you've selected it, change it to the color of your choice. You then can rotate the image into position. To add the "hole," use the Shape Path tool again to create a small black circle. To add a little more depth to my tags, I add a drop-shadow (see the directions above at right).

I've found that I learn best by taking something apart and studying it, so I was thrilled when I happened upon a couple of Web sites that have some amazing embellishments to share and tutorials for creating your own. Make sure to check out www.scrapbook-bytes.com (with a gallery and message board to boot) and www.escrappers.com.

ADDING SHADOWS

Shadows play a key role in making digital designs look realistic. In PhotoImpact, I can right-click on any object and add a shadow by selecting it from a drop-down menu. Other image-editing programs often offer something similar. Play with the adjustable variables until you get the most realistic shadow size. If you can't find an option that automatically creates a drop-shadow for your object, create a duplicate of your object by copying and pasting, change it to a dark gray or black, and then using your Layers palette, send it behind your original object. Nudge your shadow slightly down and to the right or left until it looks right. If you have the option to create a soft edge on your shadow, do so to make it look more realistic. Adding shadows to your text, photos, tags, and other embellishments is a great way to create a realistic three-dimensional effect.

KEY: Fonts

Fonts are a definite weakness of mine. I have more than 1,000 in my collection, and I don't anticipate stopping anytime soon. Possessing their own unique style, fonts can add just the right touch to your scrapbook pages.

Unfortunately, they also can slow down your computer's performance if you have too many (believe me, they can!). A font manager will give you the option of printing out all your fonts. Then go through them and select your favorites and those that you can do without. The font manager should provide a way to move or uninstall fonts that you don't use anymore or want to save to use later.

If you're looking to add more fonts to your system, search the Internet for free fonts. Or try a site like www.twopeasinabucket.com, which sells unique fonts created specifically for the site for about $2 each. You also can find hundreds of free fonts at www.scrapvillage.com, which has dedicated a portion of the Web site to fonts found all over the Web. Another site to check out is www.onescrappysite.com, which, besides providing some great fonts, also includes a tutorial on downloading fonts.

DOLLAR PARK

Our favorite place
to go when the sun
is shining.

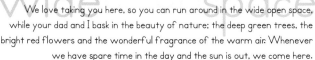

wide open space

We love taking you here, so you can run around in the wide open space,
while your dad and I bask in the beauty of nature: the deep green trees, the
bright red flowers and the wonderful fragrance of the warm air. Whenever
we have spare time in the day and the sun is out, we come here.

CREATING CUSTOM BACKGROUNDS

Creating your own background is easy with the tools available in most image-editing programs. With PhotoImpact, you can choose to fill your background (look for a paint bucket or similar icon in your program) and add any texture or color you'd like to create your background. Want to do some color-blocking? Create a path and then choose Fill to add a texture or color. If you want all your blocks the same size, just copy and paste your first block, move it to where you want it, and fill it again with a different color.

APPLYING FILTERS AND SPECIAL EFFECTS

Each image-editing program comes with its own set of filters and effects. The best way to learn about them is to spend some time playing with them. Use online resources when you need help with a technique. Do a search for tutorials using your program name and the word "tutorial." You're sure to find a wealth of information. Be advised, however, that although filters can be great, overuse can make pages appear cluttered.

We've given you a lot to digest in this quick overview, and we hope you're walking away with some new insight into the world of digital design. No matter what your skill level, there are exciting ways you can incorporate your computer into your scrapbooking projects. Whether you're a relative newbie or a computer guru, there are always new techniques to be discovered around the next corner. Enjoy!

DENISE DOCHERTY PRODUCED this computer-generated layout in Adobe Photoshop 7, creating the basic structure of the pages by using blocks of black and white. Photos were then inserted, sized, and cropped to her liking. She tilted some slightly for visual interest and faded the edge of the main photo into the foreground. Denise added her journaling in several layers for maximum flexibility in text placement.

SOURCES: COMPUTER FONTS ARE PORT CREDIT (TITLE) AND PRIMER PRINT (JOURNALING) DOWNLOADED OFF THE INTERNET. **DESIGN BY DENISE DOCHERTY.**

MORE IDEAS

Find more computer scrapbooking tips and ideas by clicking on the Exclusive Online Designs link at www.bhg.com/sipscrapbooks.

digital picks

LEARN WHAT IT WILL COST—AND WHAT YOU SHOULD LOOK FOR—TO ENTER THE WORLD OF DIGITAL PHOTOGRAPHY.

ARTICLE BY PATRICK SOLOMON

when it was suggested that I write an article about digital cameras, I was thrilled to have the opportunity. Truth be told, I haven't really been paying much attention to the technology lately. Now I had an excuse to see what's been going on in the land of megapixels.

I researched the latest releases on the digital camera market, and what I found were some outstanding values. Features that would have cost thousands of dollars a few years ago are now available for less than $500. There's also an amazing diversity in the product offerings. Whether you're a point-and-click photographer or you understand how your focal length affects your shutter speed, you'll find a camera that fits both your shooting style and your pocketbook.

UNDER $200

Even at the low end of the price scale, you'd be hard-pressed to find anything less than a 2-megapixel camera at your favorite electronics superstore. If you happen to find one with a lower resolution sitting there gathering dust on a shelf, let it be. It's there for a reason.

In this price range, you'll definitely find cameras of the point-and-shoot variety. Most of the cameras are in the 3-megapixel range. You won't be swapping out lenses or taking rapid-sequence shots with any of these. The biggest pitfall, though, may be the size of the included "digital film"—cheaper cameras frequently come equipped with slower media that can hold only a few shots at the device's highest resolution. Be sure to factor in the cost of additional storage media when comparing the costs of these cameras to some of their more expensive brethren.

$200 TO $400

Step up a little bit in price and you'll find mostly 4- and 5-megapixel cameras, more advanced controls, and the ability to add different lenses if desired. Generally, the cameras in this category power up faster (which means you can start snapping pictures faster) and need less time to recover between shots than those in the under-$200 category. At the high end of the consumer camera price range, you'll find plenty of 5-megapixel models, more photographic features you can tweak, and even a few cameras that can take quick-sequence shots. During an online search, I even found a 6-megapixel camera in this price range. Generally, a 4-megapixel camera will produce an excellent quality 8×10" print, leaving you a little room to allow for cropping. The 5-megapixel cameras and up allow for even bigger prints and more cropping room.

$600 AND ABOVE

Anything above $600 is approaching the "prosumer" category— a zone somewhere between professional and consumer photography. If you're looking to spend next year's tax refund a little early, you could head for your local electronics superstore and pick up a pro SLR with removable lenses, short shutter speeds, fast auto-focus response, and greater overall flexibility.

My suggestion? If you're just starting out, stick to the cameras under $400. Find one that matches your shooting style—that is, go ahead and pay a little more for advanced features if you already know how to use them or want to learn. At the rate this technology is advancing, by the time you're ready to replace that inexpensive camera, 13.7-megapixel models probably can be had for about $500.

megawhatzel?

Anything digital comes with its own semi-comprehensible jargon. Don't be intimidated by talk of megapixels and CCDs, though—this stuff isn't as complicated as it seems.

MEGAPIXEL: "Pixel" is short for "picture element," and a pixel is essentially a dot—which in combination with a whole lot of other dots makes a picture. "Megapixel" means 1 million pixels; therefore, a 4-megapixel camera makes up images with about 4 million dots. The more dots the better, right? Well, it's a general truth that the higher the number of megapixels, the more detail a picture will have and the better it will look when it's printed at larger sizes. For example, a 2-megapixel image printed as an 8×10" photo will look fuzzy compared to a 4-megapixel image printed at the same size. However, the number of megapixels isn't the only determining factor for image quality. If you're not happy with the image, it doesn't matter how many megapixels it has.

OPTICAL VS. DIGITAL ZOOM: When you switch from a wide-angle view to a telephoto view, you're using a camera's zoom feature. An optical zoom changes the focal length of the lens, and a digital zoom just pushes the image's pixels farther apart, which can hurt the image quality. Don't be impressed by a camera's digital-zoom capabilities; it's the optical zoom that's important.

CCD vs. CMOS: I'm not going to bore you with what these abbreviations stand for, but they are two very different ways that digital cameras capture images. If you're trying to decide between a CCD camera and a CMOS camera, the CCD model almost certainly will offer better image quality.

DIGITAL FILM: OK, I fibbed a bit in the introduction: "Digital film" really can be complicated. For one thing, it's not film. It's a magnetic storage device, somewhat akin to a floppy disk or hard drive on a computer. The problem is that there are many different and incompatible ways digital cameras can store the pictures you take. Their costs, storage capabilities, advantages, and disadvantages should be weighed before you buy a camera, because once you do, you'll be stuck using that camera's type of "film." Here are the most popular types of digital film:

- **CompactFlash.** This is commonly used in cameras; hence, there's a lot of competition among manufacturers—which helps keep the price down. An off-brand 64 MB CompactFlash card will set you back less than $20.

- **Memory Stick.** This proprietary Sony format has recently been licensed, so you'll start seeing it in more and more products. It's small, which helps keep the sizes of the cameras down, but it's also a bit slower and a lot pricier than CompactFlash. A 64 MB Memory Stick from Sony is about $50; other brands are about $40.
- **SD/MMC.** Secure Digital/Multimedia Cards also are fairly popular, but the high-capacity ones are pricier than CompactFlash cards. A 64 MB SD/MMC card costs about $25.
- **SmartMedia.** These cards didn't quite live up to their name and have been replaced by the faster and smaller xD-Picture cards. Still, they're not very expensive. A 64 MB SmartMedia card is about $25.
- **xD Picture.** This is the smallest format of the bunch. Because it's so small, it helps keep cameras small, too. A 64 MB xD Picture card costs about $25.

calling the shots

Wondering how many photos you can store on each type of storage device? There's no easy answer. The number of images you can store on any type of device depends on four factors:

1. How many megapixels the camera is capable of shooting
2. Whether the camera is set to "basic," "normal," or "fine" mode
3. The compression technique employed by the camera in each of those modes
4. The resolution the camera has been set to (sometimes shown as "large," "medium," and "small")

If you take any two 3-megapixel cameras and place 64 MB of RAM in them, they could hold vastly different numbers of pictures based on the default settings of the cameras. As you make changes to the settings, the cameras automatically update the number of pictures available on their display screens. The only thing that's for certain is that the more memory you have, the more pictures you can store.

IMPROVE YOUR

TAP INTO TECHNOLOGY TO SCAN, EDIT, AND PRINT CREATIVE PHOTOS AND GRAPHICS FOR YOUR LAYOUTS.

image

You should have seen your face when you first stuck your hand into that pumpkin! Utter disgust! There was no way I was getting you to stick your hand back into that thing! But when all was said and done, you were very impressed with the results! The look on your face when I lit the pumpkin's candle was absolutely priceless!

PUMPKIN CARVING

Jennifer Knewbow loved this photo of her son with his first carved pumpkin so much that she knew she wanted it to be the only photo on this layout. To make the pumpkin the focal point in the photo and to get rid of unwanted colors, she used Adobe Photoshop to desaturated all the color in the photo except for the pumpkin's. She kept the background clean and simple by printing her journaling on a torn strip of white vellum and using only one patterned paper, which she crumpled up and lightly dabbed with a black ink pad for an aged look. For added interest, Jennifer included a square metal-rim tag with a stamped pumpkin linked to a safety pin with "carve" spelled out in alphabet beads.

SOURCES: PATTERNED PAPER BY BO-BUNNY PRESS. COMPUTER FONT IS HELENA'S HAND, DOWNLOADED OFF THE INTERNET. PUMPKIN STAMP BY DJ INKERS. METAL-RIM TAG BY MAKING MEMORIES. **DESIGN BY JENNIFER KNEWBOW.**

GLOW
1. TO GIVE OFF A BRIGHT LIGHT
2. to be elated
3. a countenance that reflects great joy

Remember when...

you asked

M & K

M & K

Although Shannon Tidwell loved the looks of elation on the faces of her brother and his fiancée in their first engagement photo, the quality of the image wasn't up to her usual standards. To compensate for the slightly out-of-focus photo, Shannon disguised the flaws by using her computer to print it onto textured paper. With the addition of metal photo corners, the large black-and-white image became a stunning layout element.

Shannon constructed the pieced background by stapling pieces of striped and floral-print paper to the brown card stock background. She also embellished the cover of a small spiral-bound booklet with a smaller version of the black-and-white photo and a metal frame, then stapled a rubber-band title below the image. The rest of the title was written on a metal-rim tag and pinned to the rubber band with a pink safety pin.

SOURCES: PATTERNED PAPER BY KI MEMORIES. DEFINITION STICKERS, METAL PHOTO CORNERS, METAL FRAME, AND METAL LETTERS BY MAKING MEMORIES. CHARMS FROM TWO PEAS IN A BUCKET. SAFETY PIN BY LI'L DAVIS DESIGNS. WAXY FLAX BY SCRAPWORKS. BOOKLET AND RUBBER BAND BY 7GYPSIES. **DESIGN BY SHANNON TIDWELL.**

CHERISHED ROMANCE

On this page, designer Erikia Ghumm layered copies of handwritten letters, torn book pages, photographs, and other memorabilia to create a page that makes a statement about the artist. To add interest to the embossed card stock she used for the background, Erikia rubbed it with ink to bring out the patterns before layering on the duplicates of her memorabilia.

SOURCES: EMBOSSED PAPER BY K&COMPANY. CIRCLE PUNCH BY FAMILY TREASURES. METAL-RIM TAGS BY MAKING MEMORIES. BLUE BUTTERFLY, BLUE TEXT TRANSPARENCY, AND TYPEWRITER-KEY LETTERS BY ARTCHIX STUDIO. SLIDE MOUNTS BY LOERSCH. CRAFTING FOIL BY ST. LOUIS CRAFTS. RUBBER STAMPS BY HERO ARTS. METAL STAMPS BY YOUNG BROS. STAMP WORKS, INC. STAR EYELETS BY JEWELCRAFT. **DESIGN BY ERIKIA GHUMM.**

BABY BOOTIE

Inspired by the traditional hand-coloring of vintage photographs, designer Danelle Johnson created a similar look by using her computer to tint chosen areas of her photograph and then printed the image onto watercolor paper. After choosing a background paper with a graphic text pattern, she added layers of soft ribbon, fabric, and embellishments to the page. She dressed up the photo with a vintage belt buckle and sheer ribbon, then added a painted slide mount and a pressed flower sandwiched in an optical lens.

SOURCES: PATTERNED PAPER BY DANELLE JOHNSON FOR CREATIVE IMAGINATIONS. COMPUTER FONT IS LABEL MAKER POSITIVE, DOWNLOADED OFF THE INTERNET. STICKERS BY ALL MY MEMORIES (ALPHABET) AND PRESSED PETALS (FLOWER). METAL-RIM TAG BY MAKING MEMORIES. OPTICAL LENS BY ANIMA DESIGNS. CRAFT PAINT BY ART DECO. **DESIGN BY DANELLE JOHNSON.**

SOPHIE

After scanning and resizing a photo of her daughter, designer Vivian Smith printed the images on an ink-jet transparency, using the high-quality setting rather than the transparency one for better image quality. She flipped one of the images over and mounted both on white card stock trimmed to the same size as the photos. After arranging her page elements, Vivian marked the position of the photos on another transparency laid on top and then cut around them. She sprinkled the sheet with embossing powder and heat-set it, being careful to stop before the sheet warped.

SOURCES: PATTERNED PAPER BY DESIGN ORIGINALS (BLUE, RULERS, AND SCRIPT) AND PROVO CRAFT (PINK). TRANSPARENCY SHEETS BY MAGIC SCRAPS (BACKGROUND) AND 3M (PHOTOS). COMPUTER FONT IS PC RATATAT, "A GATHERING OF FRIENDS" CD BY PROVO CRAFT HUGWARE. CUTOUT LETTERS BY HOT OFF THE PRESS. METAL-RIM TAG BY SONNETS FOR CREATIVE IMAGINATIONS. HEART AND CIRCLE BRADS BY PROVO CRAFT. CHARMS BY MEMORIES IN THE MAKING. EMBOSSING POWDER BY STAMPIN' UP!. **DESIGN BY VIVIAN SMITH.**

Sophie, when I see this photo of you, my heart just melts. I love how wet your little pink tongue is and how natural & un-posed you look. When I hold you, I really feel different. I can feel how much you trust me & it really makes me love you more if that's possible.

BUTTERFLY GARDEN

After failing to capture on film the butterflies that swarmed around her and her daughter during a visit to a butterfly garden, designer Nicole Gartland decided to re-create the atmosphere with transparencies decorated with images copied from an old children's book. She printed the images on computer paper and on a transparency. Using a light box, she placed a piece of gray card stock over the paper printout, using it as a color guide as she painted the card stock with acrylic paints. Once the paint had dried, she placed the trimmed transparency on top and secured it with eyelets and ribbon.

SOURCES: COMPUTER FONTS ARE CASHMIRA (LARGE TITLE), DOWNLOADED OFF THE INTERNET AND BLUEBERRY PIE (JOURNALING) BY TWO PEAS IN A BUCKET. SLICK WRITER PENS BY AMERICAN CRAFTS. EYELETS BY MAKING MEMORIES. RIBBON BY WESTRIM CRAFTS. BUTTERFLY IMAGES FROM *CHILDREN'S GUIDE TO KNOWLEDGE* BY LEONARD J. BUCHNER. **DESIGN BY NICOLE GARTLAND.**

The zoo's butterfly garden was absolutely amazing. Everywhere we looked, a dozen (or so) varieties of butterfly perched, hung, flew and fluttered.
I loved holding very still and waiting for one to land, but Natalie couldn't quite do that. Oh, she'd try, but as soon as one would fly close, she'd duck away and giggle (which is why I don't have a single shot that contains both a butterfly and Natalie). Needless to say, this was quite adorable.
I do have hopes for our next visit though, especially because she's been looking at these pictures (while I work here) and telling me about seeing butterfies and holding very, very still.   8/2003

HAPPY VALENTINE'S DAY

Polly Maly used a picture drawn by her daughter as the focal point of this Valentine's Day card. First she reduced the image and printed it on transparency film, making sure it fit in the window of the die-cut frame. She attached a piece of patterned paper just slightly larger than the frame window to the front panel of the card. After securing the transparency to the frame on the back, she used adhesive-foam tape to attach the piece to the front panel of the card. She attached rhinestones to the frame with clear-drying glue for extra interest.

SOURCES: TWO-TONE CARD STOCK BY PAPER ADVENTURES. PATTERNED PAPER AND DIE-CUT FRAME BY PAPERFEVER. TRANSPARENCY FILM BY 3M. RHINESTONE CRYSTALS BY WESTRIM CRAFTS. **DESIGN BY POLLY MALY.**

HEY DIDDLE DIDDLE

Rather than print the photo and nursery rhyme illustration onto paper for this scrapbook page, designer Nicole Gartland added to the vintage feel of the page by printing the photos onto ink-jet–printer canvas and adding sewn and embroidered embellishments. Although ink-jet–printer canvas is specially prepared for use on a home printer, a similar effect can be achieved by securing a piece of regular fabric to a sheet of computer paper. Run the paper with the fabric attached through your printer as you would a single piece of paper, and then remove the fabric from the paper after printing and mount it on your page.

SOURCES: COMPUTER FONTS ARE SCRAP SCRIPT (TITLE) BY LETTERINGDELIGHTS AND AQUADUCT ITALIC (JOURNALING), DOWNLOADED OFF THE INTERNET. **DESIGN BY NICOLE GARTLAND.**

IT'S A SPRING THING

Even though designer Nia Reddy loved these photos of her son, Aiden, she needed to find a way to draw the eye to the main photo. In just a few clicks on her computer, Nia changed it to black-and-white and cropped and printed it in a panoramic format. She printed her title, quote, and journaling in colors slightly darker than her background paper in order to not distract from the photos. Other strips of paper, chosen to coordinate with Aiden's shirt, were added before she mounted the photo and the tag, which opens to reveal more journaling.

SOURCES: PATTERNED PAPER BY KI MEMORIES. COMPUTER FONTS ARE COPPER-PLATE (TITLE) BY APPLE AND ARIAL (JOURNALING) BY MICROSOFT. TAG BY HALLMARK. **DESIGN BY NIA REDDY.**

SAILOR

Kathleen Paneitz created this layout about her mother, the "Sailor Girl" shown in the photo. Kathleen started by scanning the small original image and enlarging it. After printing out the large version, she ran it through her printer again, so that her title and journaling were printed directly on the image. She then worked on adding a few embellishments, like a metal oval with "girl" stamped onto it and a simple round tag with a sticker saying inside. To finish the layout, Kathleen double-matted the photo with white and black card stock.

SOURCES: COMPUTER FONT IS VLADIMIR SCRIPT, DOWNLOADED OFF THE INTERNET. METAL-RIM TAG AND METAL OVAL BY MAKING MEMORIES. METAL STAMPS BY PITTSBURGH TOOLS FOR HARBOR FREIGHT. EYELETS BY CREATIVE IMAGINATIONS. ALPHABET STICKERS ARE CLASS A PEELS BY MARK ENTERPRISES. "SIMPLY IRRESISTIBLE" STICKER IS A SHOTZ THOUGHTZ BY CREATIVE IMAGINATIONS.
DESIGN BY KATHLEEN PANEITZ.

Mass Destruction & Chaos as
TYNADO hits
Parents of this little baby shake their heads in
disbelief as he wreaks havoc and destroys the
whole house in under ten minutes.
How can something this cute be so destructive?
Clean up of the event took hours only to
have the process repeated shortly after. SIGH !

TYNADO

Designer Rachel Dickson used Adobe Photoshop 7.0 to design this digital page about her son Tyler and his habit of leaving a path of destruction wherever he's playing. She included photographs of the damage done in a strip down the left side of the page that also serves as a backdrop for the title letters. The main photo of Tyler with a mischievous glint in his eye was outlined and tilted to make it stand out. Rachel also designed a three-dimensional accent positioned at the bottom of the page to drive home the tornado theme.

SOURCES: COMPUTER FONTS ARE STAMPEDE (LARGE TITLE), PROBLEM SECRETARY (SMALL TITLE), TYPEWRITER (JOURNALING), AND CALLISTO MT ("TYNADO), ALL DOWNLOADED OFF THE INTERNET. **DESIGN BY RACHEL DICKSON.**

BORN TO ROCK

When designer Margie Lundy sat down to design this page about her son's love of rock and roll, she started by converting the photos to black-and-white. She allowed a large image to dominate the upper portion of the page and placed four smaller images along the bottom edge, tinting each with a bold color. Margie also positioned the title letters over each photo, adjusting the opacity to allow the background to show through a bit.

SOURCES: INK-JET PHOTO PAPER BY HEWLETT-PACKARD. COMPUTER FONTS ARE GOUDY OLD STYLE BY ADOBE SYSTEMS AND CAC SHISHONI BRUSH, DOWNLOADED OFF THE INTERNET. **DESIGN BY MARGIE LUNDY.**

8/14/03

ROYAL TYRRELL **MUSEUM**

Amy van Engelen started this layout thinking she would make only a few dinosaur bones and a dustpan. But when she decided she wanted to create something with a "wow" effect, she downloaded a photo of a dinosaur skeleton from the Internet and used the photo to create a pattern for a three-dimensional skeleton made of card stock.

Amy cut the individual bones from dark gray card stock, shaded them with black chalk, and adhered them to her pages with adhesive foam to give dimension. She also created and affixed a broom and dustpan in the same manner. Amy based the layout color scheme on the museum brochure that provides the page title.

SOURCES: COMPUTER FONT IS TEMPUS SANS BY ITC. CHALK BY CRAF-T PRODUCTS. SKELETON, BROOM AND DUSTPAN ARE AMY'S OWN DESIGN. PATTERNS ON PAGES 94–95. **DESIGN BY AMY VAN ENGELEN.**

SAVTA

An old photo of Lilac Chang's grandmother became a personal treasure when she discovered it in one of her mother's albums. She decided to preserve it in a layout that features colors, patterns, and textures she felt represented the Middle East, where her family originated.

To avoid damaging the original image, she used a scanned version printed on watercolor paper. For the background, she layered patterned papers and pieces of fabric, adhering them with spray adhesive. After placing the image on top of a black envelope, she added a strip of rubber-stamped fabric, inked metal letters, and a metal brooch. The page's journaling is inside the small booklet she mounted on the page. After printing the text on a long strip of card stock, she folded the piece in half, decorated the front with more card stock and fabric, and added a printed transparency.

SOURCES: PATTERNED PAPER FROM SONNETS BY CREATIVE IMAGINATIONS (BEIGE PAISLEY) AND KAREN FOSTER DESIGN (ORANGE-AND-RED BRUSHSTROKE). RUBBER STAMPS BY AMERICAN ART STAMP (SCRIPT), THE RUBBERNECKER STAMP CO. (ON PAISLEY PAPER), AND JUDIKINS (ON ORANGE FABRIC). METAL LETTERS BY MAKING MEMORIES. BROWN BRADS BY LOST ART TREASURES FOR AMERICAN TAG CO. RIVETS BY CHATTERBOX. PRINTED TRANSPARENCY BY MAGIC SCRAPS. BLACK ENVELOPE FROM TWO PEAS IN A BUCKET. **DESIGN BY LILAC CHANG.**

FOR YOU, DAD, FROM YOUR DAUGHTER

Designed by Tristann Graves—the little girl in the picture who is now fully grown—this layout is a tribute to time spent together by father and daughter. Tristann recognized the scrapbooking possibilities of a vellum overlay saved from an old Hallmark card and wanted to make use of it on this page. Because it was already printed with the words shown, all Tristann needed to do was scan and resize several snapshots of her and her father and place them in the openings. She topped the page with a length of wired ribbon gathered in spots with golden star-shape nailheads.

SOURCES: PATTERNED PAPERS BY K&COMPANY (PHOTO MAT) AND PAPER PIZAZZ FOR HOT OFF THE PRESS (BACKGROUND). COMPUTER FONTS ARE FORMAL 436 (TEXT IN TAG) AND DELLA ROBBIA (QUOTE) BY BITSTREAM. PRINTED VELLUM AND TAG DIE CUT BY PAPER PIZAZZ FOR HOT OFF THE PRESS. DAD STICKER BY PSX. WIRED RIBBON BY CURRENT. NAILHEADS BY WESTRIM. HEART CHARM BY HALCRAFT. PHOTO CORNERS BY PIONEER. **DESIGN BY TRISTANN GRAVES.**

WHEN I'M GONE

Shannon Miklo created this page as a way to express some of her sadness over her husband's three-month deployment. Using digital photos of her husband and daughter saying good-bye and reuniting with a kiss, Shannon created this layout on her computer using Adobe Photoshop 7.0. By working with opacity levels, she was able to create a realistic-looking transparency held in place with computer-generated eyelets. To make the eyelets and layers seem more realistic, she used shadow and bevel effects on those pieces. Shannon also used filters and special effects to create the textured background.

SOURCES: COMPUTER FONT IS GARAMOND BY MICROSOFT. **DESIGN BY SHANNON MIKLO.**

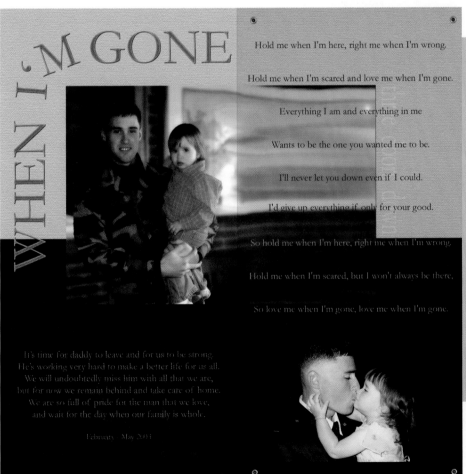

COUSINS

katelyn & kayla ♥

Although Katelyn and Kayla don't get to see each other very often, they have a special connection as cousins and always had a great time when they do get together. Each visit takes its initial few warming up moments, but then they're off, whether it's jumping on the bed, chasing Grant or finding treasures in Grandma & Grandpa's rocks. This was one of the last photos they took together before we moved to California, and they moved back to Lincoln from Washington!

photos taken Summer 2002

COUSINS
KATELYN & KAYLA

Anita Matejka used photo-editing software to create frames on the photo of her daughters on this layout. She also changed some portions of the photo to black-and-white, while leaving the center of the image in color to further accentuate their faces. Computer embossing doesn't actually emboss your photo but rather adds shading to the image to simulate the look.

SOURCES: COMPUTER FONT IS TYPEWRITER BY AGFA MONOTYPE. ALPHABET STICKERS ARE SONNETS BY SHARON SONEFF FOR CREATIVE IMAGINATIONS. METAL HEARTS BY MAKING MEMORIES (HEAT-EMBOSSED WITH WHITE POWDER). FIBERS ARE ADORNAMENTS BY EK SUCCESS. **DESIGN BY ANITA MATEJKA.**

CREATIVE ALTERNATIVES

If you're squeamish about embossing your photos, there are alternatives to achieve a similar effect. Many photo-editing programs can be used to create the illusion of embossing on a photo. In Adobe Photoshop, the embossing option can be found in the Filter menu under Stylize, but other photo-editing programs may list it in an Effects menu or elsewhere. In many programs, you can choose from different embossing options and select the style and depth of the embossing.

THE GREAT MAN

When assembling this layout about what a great father her husband is, Anita Matejka wanted to use as many photos as possible to show off his traits. She scanned her photos and reduced them, and then she cropped them to same-size squares to create a photo mosaic. Using patterned paper with a repeated block theme, she decided on soft colors that wouldn't distract from the black-and-white pictures. For her page title, Anita used a preprinted quote sticker and mounted it on top of a block collage that ties in the design at the bottom of the page.

SOURCES: PATTERNED PAPER BY SEI. COMPUTER FONT IS SALVAGED, DOWNLOADED OFF THE INTERNET. QUOTE STICKER BY WORDSWORTH. DESIGN BY ANITA MATEJKA.

> THE GREAT MAN IS HE WHO DOES NOT LOSE HIS CHILD'S HEART.
> *mencius*

When it comes to being a father, your dad is one of the best out there! He spends most of his spare moments with you guys. When he could be golfing or watching TV or just doing something for himself, he doesn't even think twice to instead spend that time with you. Many times he will take you to the zoo by himself, even when the zoo is 2 hours away! And when we've had to decide about his career, his time spent at home was always his main concern. The best thing is that he is pretty much a kid at heart. He loves to sword fight with you, Grant, and play hide-and-seek with you, Katelyn. He's great at being silly and always has a goofy moment up his sleeve for you! I love that our house is filled with so many silly, fun, and goofy times, and Daddy is the one usually the initiator of those moments!

wonder**FALL**

family fun

Fall 2003 was a hectic time for us with Terry in Japan for 2 weeks and missing Halloween, his favorite holiday. So we made sure to take advantage of fall's fun activities and gorgeous weather while he was here . . . even if that meant carving our jack-o-lantern in November!

Bountiful Blessings

WONDER FALL

During the fall of 2003, Lisa Storm's husband was in Japan for two weeks, separated from his family during his favorite time of year. So the family celebrated Halloween when they could, visiting a pumpkin patch and carving a jack-o'-lantern in November. Lisa let the photos take center stage on this layout by keeping her embellishments to a minimum. She also accentuated each photo by mounting a cropped and matted color photograph onto a black-and-white duplicate. Then she created her title by printing a portion onto patterned paper and adding vellum sticker letters to complete it. A subtitle, framed by a metal-rim tag, balances the elements of the layout.

SOURCES: CARD STOCK BY BAZZILL BASICS PAPER. PATTERNED PAPER BY K&COMPANY. COMPUTER FONT IS CALISTO BY AGFA MONOTYPE. ALPHABET STICKERS BY MRS. GROSSMAN'S (VELLUM) AND CHATTERBOX (WHITE). WOVEN LABEL BY ME AND MY BIG IDEAS. LEAF CHARM AND METAL-RIM TAG BY MAKING MEMORIES. DESIGN BY LISA STORM.

ON THE ROAD AGAIN

Stacey Yoder wanted to create a travel page to chronicle the details of her three children's attitudes during the long drive from their hometown of Yucaipa, California, to the Colorado River. Repeated on the layout, the fitting phrase "Are we there yet?" sums up how the children were feeling.

To highlight the travel route, Stacey scanned a section of a road map and printed it on beige card stock. She then circled the starting and ending points of the trip with a red marker and traced the stretch of highway between the two points. A transparency overlay printed with black text and travel signs provides the title and the dreaded question and is secured to the page with a matted square mini brad in each corner. Miniature photos of the children, with tiny letter tiles attached, add a playful touch.

SOURCES: CARD STOCK BY BAZZILL BASICS PAPER. PRINTED TRANSPARENCY BY ARTISTIC EXPRESSIONS. COMPUTER FONT IS TIMES BY ADOBE. LETTER TILES BY LIMITED EDITION RUBBERSTAMPS. STAMP INK BY STAMPIN' UP! METAL-RIM TAG BY MAKING MEMORIES. **DESIGN BY STACEY YODER.**

SIGNS OF THE TIME

Danelle Johnson used photographs of signs taken after September 11, 2001, as the main design element on this layout about her feelings after the terrorist attacks in the United States. She used Microsoft Picture It! to manipulate the four smaller photos, giving each an artistic border. The panoramic photo in the center flips down to reveal her journaling.

SOURCES: PATTERNED PAPER BY COLORBÖK (RED), MUSTARD MOON (STARS), AND CAROLEE'S CREATIONS (BLUE STRIPE). COMPUTER FONTS ARE PAPYRUS ("OF THE") AND DISTRESS ("SIGNS" AND "TIME"), DOWNLOADED OFF THE INTERNET. **DESIGN BY DANELLE JOHNSON.**

2003

Sometimes it's good to put all of your **eggs** In one basket

Easter Egg Hunting
Easter Sunday
Grammy's House

EGGS IN ONE BASKET

Designer Sam Cousins found that the best way to deal with the clashing colors of her son Ben's Easter outfit and the Easter eggs was to digitally remove the color from the photos and then selectively add color back in on the basket and eggs. The result was a dramatic photo, highlighting the rainbow of egg hues in the basket and the single egg Ben holds in his hand.

SOURCES: COMPUTER FONT IS DEAR DIARY BY TWO PEAS IN A BUCKET. PAGE PEBBLES ARE SONNETS BY CREATIVE IMAGINATIONS. BRADS BY MAKING MEMORIES. JEWELRY TAGS FROM STAPLES. FIBERS BY FIBERS BY THE YARD. **DESIGN BY SAM COUSINS.**

TRACES OF YOU

After gathering photos of herself and her mother for this layout, designer Anita Matejka needed to find a way to give the photos a cohesive look. To overcome the differences in photo quality, age, and color, she scanned each one so she could edit the images digitally. Using a photo-editing program, Anita scanned, cropped, and resized them and added a creative brushstroke frame around each photo. She printed the edited images on vellum, tore the edges, and matted each with blue torn-edge card stock. Tags of different sizes and shapes gave her several options for labeling the photos.

SOURCES: PATTERNED PAPER IS SHARON ANN COLLECTION BY DEJA VIEWS. COMPUTER FONT IS FALLING LEAVES BY TOWPEASINABUCKET.COM. BUTTONS BY MAKING MEMORIES. FIBERS BY RUBBA DUB DUB. MESH BY MAGIC SCRAPS. ALBUM BY KOLO. **DESIGN BY ANITA MATEIKA.**

DANCES WITH SONG KID

Nicole Gartland's daughter loves Shirley Temple—"Song Kid" as she's known around the Gartland home—and asks her mother to play a tape of her song-and-dance numbers daily. Natalie isn't content to merely watch the tape, however, and joins in by twirling, tapping, and singing along.

When Nicole sat down to document this aspect of her daughter's personality, she relied heavily on her image-editing software. She sketched Shirley Temple doodles in the same poses as her daughter in the photos, silhouetted the photos and the doodles, and placed them on a sheet of white paper. Then she scanned them into her image-editing program. She adjusted the scans to give them the "sketch" quality shown and used red ink to print them on teal card stock.

SOURCES: PATTERNED PAPER BY COLORS BY DESIGN. COMPUTER FONTS ARE MECHANICAL FUN (WORDS WITH LINES), ACORN SQUASH ALTERNATIVE (NAMES AND LARGE TITLE WORDS), GLOBALHEAD ("WITH"), AND NIGMA (JOURNALING), DOWNLOADED OFF THE INTERNET. PUNCHES BY MARVY UCHIDA (LARGE STAR) AND FISKARS (SMALL STAR). **DESIGN BY NICOLE GARTLAND.**

beyond the box

USE YOUR COMPUTER TO JOURNAL INSIDE CIRCLES AND ALONG CURVES TO GIVE YOUR PAGES NEW LIFE AND HELP YOU BREAK OUT OF THE JOURNALING BOX.

ARTICLE AND DESIGN BY ERIN TERRELL

each year, in an attempt to reflect

the energy of the springtime world around me, I tend to reach for brighter colors of patterned paper to match the vibrant hues of the season. Sometimes, however, a change in papers just isn't enough. Lately I've been playing with the arrangement of my photos, titles, and journaling blocks as well. I've discovered that it's fun to shake things up a bit and not stick with the old tried-and-true scrapbooking formulas.

For example, who says journaling needs to be contained in a block that will fit the empty space between photos? It's time to break out of that boring box. Try journaling in circles or swirls for a change. It's fun and easy to do using your computer.

GETTING INTO THE GROOVE

If you have a computer, you probably have access to the popular word-processing program Microsoft Word. It's a great program for typing documents, and it also has some lesser-known graphic capabilities. Follow these steps to create circular text using Microsoft Word.

1. Open a new document. You will need to have the WordArt toolbar visible on your screen. To do this, select View from the menu options at the top of the screen. From the drop-down menu, select Toolbars. Then, from the choices offered, put a check mark next to WordArt. The toolbar will look similar to the one *below*—the appearance may vary slightly depending on which version of Microsoft Word you are running.

2. Click on the tilted blue "A." This will pull up the WordArt function, which allows you to create unusual text effects.

3. Select the 3rd WordArt style from the top left and click "OK." The text shape will resemble a rainbow. See the image *below*.

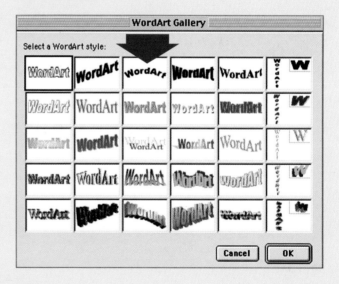

4. Next, choose a font and type size. Type the text in the space provided, and click "OK." The text you have chosen will appear on your document with white squares in each corner.

ERIN PRINTED her title and journaling for this layout on vellum using Microsoft Word. She trimmed the vellum circle with black card stock and used flower-shape brads to attach the circle to the page. The flowers and stems were cut using a template, and buttons were added to the flower centers for dimension.

SOURCES: Textured paper by Solum World Papers. Patterned paper, Funky Bradletz, and flower and stem template by Provo Craft. Computer fonts are Jayne (journaling) and Brotherman (title), downloaded off the Internet. Buttons by Magic Scraps.

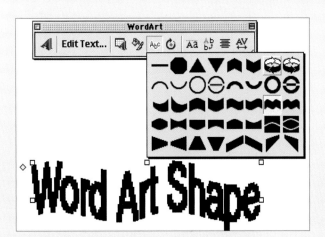

5. On the WordArt menu, choose the WordArt Shape button. This button will allow you to choose the shape of your text. Select the circle, and your text will appear in a circular shape. You can then "tug" at the little white boxes in each corner of the text to change the size of the circle.

When you use this method to create a circular title, choose a fairly bold and easy-to-read font. Also, longer titles with lots of words look best in this title style—it's difficult to make a circle out of a short word!

To further vary the look of your layout, try showcasing the title by swirling it across the page. In Word, open the WordArt toolbar. Select the WordArt style bar that appears as a wavy shape, and design a title.

In addition to Microsoft Word, other computer programs can create circular titles. Chatterbox (a division of EK Success) makes a program called Journaling Genie that allows users to type text in circles or swirls by selecting one of many available shapes.

Whether you use a basic word-processing program or more sophisticated illustration software, don't be afraid to experiment with type. Consider using curved and wavy lines on a sailing layout to suggest waves, on a layout where a child is swinging to represent wind action, or on a wintry layout to simulate wind blowing through a scene. Journaling in a circle or swirl may be just the whimsical touch you're looking for.

font of information

SCRAPBOOKERS INTERESTED IN CREATING CUSTOM FONTS HAVE A VARIETY OF OPTIONS.

ARTICLE BY PATRICK SOLOMON

my handwriting is so bad, my mother told me I should have become a doctor. Fortunately, with the advent of word processing, my poor script never became an issue. Everyone can read my typing, thanks to standard typefaces known as fonts.

If you don't work in the publishing industry, you probably never even heard the word "font" until you bought your first computer. Your basic home computer comes with dozens of typefaces to choose from, but if you're like most computer users, you probably use only two or three on a regular basis. "There are thousands and thousands of fonts out there," says Melissa Baxter, who has created approximately two hundred fonts for the scrapbooking Web site www.twopeasinabucket.com.

If your perfect font doesn't exist, though, you've got a couple of options: Either find a designer who can make custom fonts for you, or buy some software that will help you make your own fonts.

Why would you want to create your own font? Perhaps you'd like to turn your handwriting or the handwriting of a loved one into a font. Or maybe you just saw a type treatment in print and you'd like to be able to use it in your projects. "Most scrapbookers find fonts that they like in magazines," Baxter says.

Unfortunately, you can't just look up "Fonts" in the Yellow Pages to find a designer. Fortunately, you *can* find plenty of them on the Internet.

Fontgod.com (www.fontgod.com/index.htm), based in Coffs Harbour, Australia, can create custom TrueType fonts within five business days for as little as $45.95 USD. The fonts might be based on your own handwriting, provided to Fontgod.com via a template you download, or on handwriting you've found on an old document—a letter written by a great-grandparent, for example. However, the company cannot convert cursive or connected writing into fonts, so be sure to check the samples page to see what the fonts look like.

If you're feeling particularly creative, software is available that can help you create your own fonts. It's not a simple process, but it's not beyond your reach if you're detail-oriented and you have the time to learn a new computer program. You can spend next to nothing to nearly $1,000 on these programs, depending on how often you're planning on creating fonts and your level of interest.

If you just want to dabble, try **High-Logic's Font Creator** program (www.high-logic.com, free for 30 days and $65 for

WITH FONTLAB'S SCANFONT, scrapbookers can make their own handwriting and specialty fonts by modifying existing type or scanning in characters.

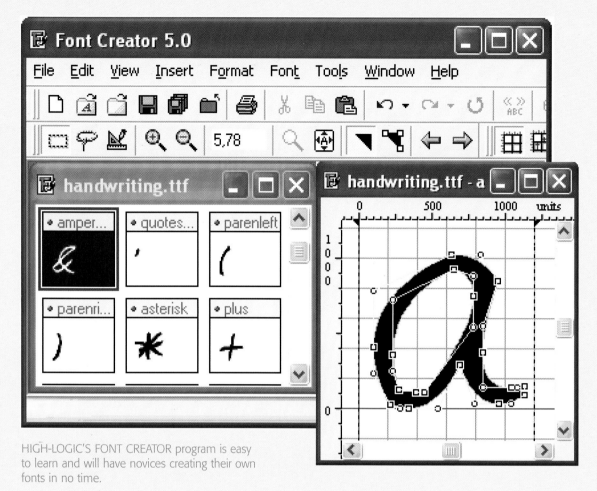

HIGH-LOGIC'S FONT CREATOR program is easy to learn and will have novices creating their own fonts in no time.

unlimited use). Novices should try altering an existing font to get a feel for the program before creating a font from scratch. Once you get the hang of it, you can import scanned images to make your own symbol fonts or, if you have a scanner, you can make your own handwriting font. The Font Creator 5 Home Edition program requires Windows 95 or later.

FontLab's ScanFont (www.pyrus.com/Font-tools/ScanFont, $199, trial versions available) "can turn almost anything into a font," the Web site boasts. You can scan a page of text, load it into ScanFont, and the software will automatically sort out the different characters. You can edit individual characters and set letter spacing and kerning pairs. The Web site includes a tutorial, which should help you get started if you have the program or figure out whether it's too complicated for you if you don't have the program. ScanFont 4 requires Mac OS X or later. ScanFont Version 3 is for Windows.

Whether you buy or create your own fonts, your pages will look their best when you pick the right font for the job. Since my handwriting is illegible at any size, I won't be turning it into a font anytime soon—but for certain projects, a custom font may add that extra dash of personality you're seeking.

Font Jargon

When working with fonts, you may run across some of these technical terms:

SERIF FONT: A font with short lines that extend from the top and bottom edges of most letters. Times New Roman is a serif font—if you look at the character "T," you'll notice the lines that descend from the top and extend from the base.

SANS SERIF FONT: A font that lacks those short lines. **Arial** is a sans serif font.

PITCH: The number of characters in one inch of print.

FIXED-WIDTH FONT: A font whose characters are each the same width. Fixed-width fonts are fairly rare (most fonts are proportional width). `Courier` is a fixed-width font.

POINT: A measure of the size of a font. Technically, a "point" is $1/72$ of an inch—so if you type something in 72-point type, its tallest characters should be an inch tall when printed. Depending on the font you're using, it may not exactly equal an inch.

WEIGHT: A measure of the thickness of a font. Bold characters "weigh" more than normal characters.

X-HEIGHT: The distance from the baseline of a line of type to the top of the main body of a lowercase letter.

ASCENDER: The upward vertical stroke on some lowercase letters—such as h, b, and d—that extends above the x-height.

DESCENDER: The "tail" on some lowercase letters—such as g, y, and j—that extends or descends below the baseline.

GEAR & GADGETS

SIMPLIFYING THE TECHNICAL JARGON MAKES CHOOSING
THE RIGHT COMPUTER, PRINTER, AND SCANNER FOR YOUR
DIGITAL SCRAPBOOKING NEEDS EASIER.

ARTICLE BY PATRICK SOLOMON

COMPUTER SCIENCE

Computer makers bombard us with numbers and acronyms that don't mean much to most folks. All that talk of gigabytes, gigahertz, and gigaflops is meant to impress you or lull you into spending more than you should. The fact is that computer speed has outpaced the ability of most applications to do something useful with that speed. Put another way, every new computer on the market today—whether it costs $500 or $3,500—is fast enough to do what you need it to do.

Here's an explanation of some of the gobbledygook you see when you're at a computer store and what you need to pay attention to if you're going to be using your new computer for typical scrapbook-related activities such as constructing layouts and printing digital photographs.

"AMD Athlon™ XP processor 2600+ with QuantiSpeed™ architecture (QuantiSpeed™ architecture operates at 2.13 GHz)"

PROCESSOR SPEED

Essentially two manufacturers make the "brains" for Windows-based personal computers these days: Intel (with chips named Celeron and Pentium 4) and AMD (with chips named Duron and Athlon). Both companies offer a variety of products at different speeds—measured in gigahertz (GHz)—that match different price points. Obviously, the processor you get in a $500 computer won't be as feature-packed or fast as one in a computer that costs seven times as much.

For everyday tasks such as e-mail, Web browsing, word processing, and the like, any processor will do. The Celeron and Duron chips are low-end processors, found in less-expensive machines, but they are plenty fast enough for most tasks. If you're going to be spending much of your time manipulating large digital photographs and laying out a lot of scrapbook pages, you might be happier going for the more advanced Pentium 4 or Athlon chips.

As for speed, there's only one general rule: Never buy the fastest chip available, because the second-fastest one will always give you more bang for the buck. These days, though, you can't go wrong with a new computer at any speed—so don't be intimidated by all the gigahertz talk. Just buy the fastest processor available at the price you want to pay.

"512 MB PC2100 DDR SDRAM for multitasking power, expandable to 1.0 GB"

RAM

The short-term storage space used by your computer is nearly as important as its processor. RAM feeds the processor with a steady stream of data, allowing your computer to work more efficiently.

Unfortunately, there are a bunch of different kinds of RAM out there, with an alphabet soup of acronyms (DDR, SD, RD, ECC, etc.) and a variety of speed ratings (PC 133, PC 2100, PC 2700, PC 4000, etc.). Fortunately, capacity is much more important than specifications. No matter what kind of RAM fits in your computer—and the store where you buy it will know what kind of RAM it takes—make sure that you've got at least 256 megabytes when you walk out the door. More is fine and less might do, but that's a good amount for strong performance.

"Seagate 40.0 GB UATA-100 5400 RPM 8.9 MS 2 MB"

HARD DRIVE

That's a whole lot of numbers to describe a computer's long-term storage space. The one number you need to be most concerned with is the one before the GB (gigabytes)—in this case, 40. That's a measure of the amount of stuff you can put on the hard drive.

If you're planning on storing a lot of pictures, clip art, or layouts on your computer, you'll need a hard drive with a large capacity. Although 40 GB is on the low end of today's storage options, that's still a lot of space. You can get 120 GB or more if you're willing to pay for it. A good compromise is 60 GB. Don't worry about the other numbers. Just pay attention to the hard drive's capacity and you'll be fine.

"48×12×48 CD-RW Drive"

OPTICAL STORAGE

The three numbers in front of the drive specification above—48×12×48—give you an idea of how fast the drive will read CD information, write to CD-RW discs, and write to CD-R discs. These numbers can range from 32×4×4 to 54×32×54. Bigger is almost certainly better.

The four basic types of optical drives are: CD (which reads audio and data CDs); CD-RW (which reads and writes audio and data CDs); DVD (which reads audio and data CDs and also reads video and data DVDs); and DVD-RW (which reads and writes audio and data CDs and reads and writes video and data DVDs).

The most problematic of these are the DVD-RW drives. Competing standards are not always interoperable, so you may not be able to share data with other computers unless they have a drive made by the same manufacturer. Plus, the video DVDs that they create aren't always readable by the DVD player you've got in your living room. Add in the high cost of blank DVDs, and you've got a technology that you probably want to stay away from for the time being.

Many computers come standard with a CD-RW drive, which is what you want. They can write to both CD-R (writable once) and CD-RW (writable over and over again) discs, and the discs themselves are relatively inexpensive.

Whether you're buying your first computer or buying one for the first time in a few years, be prepared for sticker shock—but in a good way. Ignore the hype and stick to your budget, and you'll walk away happy with your purchase.

BUYING IT

There are a couple of curiosities to ponder when picking out a new computer. The first is that computers are almost invariably made from commodity parts. Much like finding Mitsubishi engines in cars built by both Mitsubishi and Chrysler, you might find a hard drive made by Seagate in computers built by both Sony and Dell. Those drives are going to perform the same in both computers.

The other curiosity is that no matter what a computer costs, if it works flawlessly for a few weeks, it will probably keep working that way for a few years. Although some companies have better reputations for functional computers than others (Dell, Sony, and Apple tend to top consumer polls), a brand-name or high-dollar investment is no guarantee that your computer will even work right out of the box.

Problems tend to make themselves evident quickly, so be sure to exercise your warranty at the first sign of trouble.

A PRINTER PRIMER

There's something oddly intangible about the tangible. You may have the best-looking layout on your computer screen, but it just isn't the same as having the best-looking layout in your hands.

To get that layout off of your computer screen and into your hands—while maintaining its "best-looking" status—you need a quality printer. You could use someone else's quality printer by taking your computer files to a local copy shop, but it's possible to get some amazing prints at home with the latest generation of ink-jet printers. When buying a new ink-jet printer, however, keep in mind several things.

COST ISN'T JUST ABOUT THE STICKER PRICE.
Printers are sold in much the same way as razors—it's relatively cheap to purchase a razor, but the razor company more than makes up for it by selling you the razor blades for years to come. In the case of printers, the company makes a killing by selling you the ink cartridges.

DON'T BE SWAYED BY A SALE PRICE on a printer
without also checking out the price of its ink. Without the ink, the printer is useless—so make sure the cartridges are available and within your budget. Compare cartridges based on the number of pages they can produce. A $15 cartridge that yields 350 pages (4.3 cents per page) is not a better deal than a $20 cartridge that yields 500 pages (4 cents per page).

THE OTHER PRICE "GOTCHA" WITH PRINTERS.
Most don't come with a cable to connect the printer to your computer. Figure on another $10 to $20 if you need one; check the printer's box to be sure.

"MORE" IS "MORE EXPENSIVE." What's the
difference between a $79 printer and a $379 printer? Pretty much every specification possible. You'll pay more if you want more pages per minute, larger media capacities, higher resolution, and the ability to print on larger paper.

Chances are you won't need the top-of-the-line model that does everything well. If you're willing to make compromises (on, say, the amount of paper you can have stuffed in the printer at any one time), you can get a great price for the options that matter to you the most (like speed).

Buy a printer you can actually use. Bear in mind that when you get it home, you're going to have to connect your new ink-jet printer to a computer. If the printer doesn't come with the cables that fit your computer, or software that will run on your computer, then you've just bought an expensive paperweight. If you're unsure, ask.

Also—assuming the store will let you and it has on display the model you're considering—bring in the kind of paper you plan to use. If the printer jams on your heavy-weight archival paper, you need to pick a different printer.

Don't buy it if you don't like the print quality. It sounds obvious, but it really isn't. You should never buy a printer without examining some pages it has printed. There's a certain amount of subjectivity involved; if you don't think a printer reproduces flesh tones very well, it doesn't matter what kind of resolution it says it has or how much it costs.

There are two good ways to test a printer. For text, print a page full of the smallest text possible—if the letters don't smudge together, you've got a winner. For images, print one picture with good color contrast, one with a large area of a single color in various shades, and a black-and-white image. If the printer can reproduce the vibrancy of the first image, offers colors that don't look blotchy in the second one, and can faithfully print all the shades of gray in the last one, it's a keeper.

A printer won't always handle both text and images equally well. Scrapbooking projects obviously rely heavily on image quality, but if your printer also will be used for newsletters and calendars, the text quality has to be up to snuff.

People don't put much thought into buying ink-jet printers because they're relatively cheap compared to other computer peripherals. If you're willing to "kick the tires" when looking for a printer, you'll be much happier with the quality of your digitally generated scrapbook pages.

THE INSIDE SCOOP

WHAT ABOUT THOSE CHEAP INK-CARTRIDGE REFILL KITS?
You won't void your printer's warranty by using a refurbished cartridge, but the manufacturer doesn't have to agree to make repairs stemming from the use of refill kits, either. For every story I've heard about people using refills successfully for years, I've heard of another person who had to buy a new printer after getting cheap ink all over the place. Use these at your own risk.

SHOULD I GET A PRINTER THAT HOLDS TWO, FOUR, OR SIX INK CARTRIDGES?
A two-cartridge printer has one for black ink and one for all the other colors (cyan, magenta, and yellow). The big problem is that if you run out of one of the colors, you've got to replace all of the colors. With four-cartridge printers, you have to replace only the color that you've run out of. A six-cartridge printer uses light cyan and light magenta to better reproduce colors in photographs. Given a choice, I'd definitely go for a printer that holds either four or six ink cartridges—but don't pay extra for a six-cartridge machine if you find a four-cartridge model that prints images with the quality you like.

WHAT ABOUT PRINTERS THAT DOUBLE AS FAX MACHINES/SCANNERS/COPIERS?
If space is an issue, a multifunction unit might be for you. These machines are becoming increasingly popular and are available at office superstores and other mass merchants. Prices on these all-in-one units have plunged, making them a great value even if your scanner goes on the blink. With prices as low as $150, you won't sweat replacing it if it should break.

WOULD I BE BETTER OFF WITH A COLOR LASER PRINTER?
A color laser printer definitely will be faster than a color ink-jet printer, but there are two problems. First, the quality of the images isn't as good as you might think—so definitely insist on seeing printouts before buying. Second, even the cheapest color laser printer will set you back about $1,000, and you'll still have to buy toner for it.

SCANNER SAVVY

The shoe box is the undisputed king of picture storage. But as those who have made the leap to digital photography know, storing images on your computer is much handier. And if you haven't yet invested in a digital camera, the best way to get pictures from the shoe box to the hard drive is by using a scanner.

Buying a scanner is simple and can be remarkably inexpensive. Every new scanner currently on the market is capable of delivering a good image to your printer (assuming you don't have a $5,000 printer, in which case the price of the scanner probably isn't a concern).

So what's the difference between a $50 scanner and a $1,050 scanner? The technical gobbledygook separating the two is significant, but you should never buy any computer device based on numbers that the manufacturer hopes you don't understand anyway. Instead, buy a product that fits your needs. In this case, if the $50 scanner fits your needs as well as the $1,050 one, save the extra $1,000. The three major factors to consider when purchasing a scanner are resolution, scanning area, and accessories. Once you understand these features, you'll be better able to decide which scanner best suits your needs.

RESOLUTION

Scanner specifications include two important numbers: optical resolution and interpolated resolution. The optical resolution is really all you should be interested in; it's the only way to make an apples-to-apples comparison between models.

Generally speaking, the more money you pay, the better resolution you'll get. Scanners costing less than $100 tend to have a 600- or 1200-dpi (dots per inch) resolution, which means they pick up 600 or 1200 dots' worth of information in every linear inch of the picture being scanned. (If you see two numbers listed, such as "600×1200 dpi," the smaller number is the important one.) Scanners in a slightly higher price range may have 2400-dpi resolution. More dots translate into a clearer image, especially when enlarging photos.

SCANNING AREA

Nearly every scanner available is capable of scanning a sheet of 8½×11" paper, which means almost every scanner out there can scan an 8×10" photo.

If you need to scan legal-size documents (8½×14"), prepare to shell out for the privilege. In this category, $500 is typical. On the plus side, many of these scanners feature 2400-dpi resolution, can preview your scan in just four seconds, and work with both Windows and Macintosh systems. For those of you who think size really does matter, you have options—but they aren't for the faint of heart. Professional-level, extra-large scanners that allow you to scan documents up to 12×17" will put you over the $1,000 mark.

ACCESSORIES

Some scanners can be fitted with automatic sheet feeders, which allow you to scan multiple documents in a row without aligning each of them on the scanner. Although it may be tempting to dump your shoe box into a sheet feeder, try to avoid this; automatic feeders can bend or even damage photos.

A more attractive accessory might be a transparency adapter. This handy unit will scan slides and negatives as well as transparencies. For those who have carousels filled with slides, this feature can be a godsend.

As you can see, it doesn't take a large investment to bridge the gap between your shoe box and your computer. Just make sure that you buy only what you need, and avoid being intimidated by all the numbers.

digital development

WITH THE CLICK OF A MOUSE, YOU CAN HAVE YOUR DIGITAL IMAGES PROCESSED INTO HIGH-QUALITY PHOTOS.

ARTICLE BY PATRICK SOLOMON

SHUTTERFLY is one of several user-friendly online developing services, offering prints, CD archiving, online sharing, and personalized gifts.

let's say

you just dropped a lot of money on a spiffy digital camera. Your pictures look absolutely fabulous on your computer screen. However, your ink-jet printer—which dates back to the Mesozoic era—tends to reproduce your wonderful photos in the style of Renoir or, even worse, Pollock.

What can you do to keep your scrapbook pages from looking like modern art projects? You've got a couple of choices: You can spend some cash upgrading to a fabulous photo printer, or you can have your digital pictures "developed" professionally—without leaving your house. Online developing also is a great way to share photographs with far-flung friends and relatives. Nearly every online developer allows you to create virtual photo albums, which are available on the developer's Web site. The developers encourage you to share these albums, since they make money if your friends order a picture of yours, too.

Daniel Tschudi of Loretto, Minnesota, has had his digital pictures printed professionally for more than a year. "I can easily pick photos that I would like to share with friends, neighbors, and family through a basic Web interface,"

winkflash ;) ™

already a member?
⊙ **Log In**

: pricing : get started : faq : testimonials : quality : about us : contact us : pros : policies

paramount quality

Photo Development
Our #1 priority is making sure your prints meet the highest quality standards. Our digital laboratory uses premium Fuji Crystal Archive paper and chemistry, guaranteeing brighter colors, sharper whites, and prints that will last a lifetime.

Greeting, Note, and Postcards
Your cards are created using a high-quality, full color offset print process. We use 100 lb durable card-stock to make your cards exactly like those you might find at your local card store.

Shipping
We have taken extra steps to ensure that your prints arrive to you safely and undamaged. We use extra thick, stay-flat envelopes and boxes to get your photos to you as quickly and as safe as possible. Our laboratory operates 24/7 to ensure timely shipping of your prints.

Guarantee
We back all orders with a money-back guarantee, so you can feel safe that your photos will be of the highest quality.

FUJIFILM

International Sites: United Kingdom | Canada | Europe

Free Image Editing Software

WINKFLASH offers high-quality online photo developing at a very economical price, plus online storage space for sharing your images with friends and family.

Tschudi says of his favorite online developer, Shutterfly. "My friends and family can then choose photos to order. In addition, I will oftentimes have photos framed and sent to myself or other family members as gifts."

Ready to share your digital photos? Here are three online developers with slightly different ways of handling your images, and each with slightly different services and prices.

SHUTTERFLY (www.shutterfly.com)

Tschudi's choice for online developing is one of the more user-friendly services. You can choose to upload your pictures individually by browsing for them on your computer or, after downloading a small program, you can drag and drop images onto the Shutterfly site to upload them.

Once they're there, Shutterfly's software will automatically make a few adjustments to enhance the color and exposure. (If you're happy with your picture as it is, you can turn this enhancement off—but it's a nice touch.)

It's incredibly easy to crop, change colors, soften the focus, and correct red-eye on your pictures before ordering.

The biggest advantage is that you can add a border to your image to create a card, calendar, or instant scrapbook enhancer—at no additional cost. There are dozens of templates to choose from, and the quality and originality are superb.

WAL-MART PHOTO CENTER (www.walmart.com)

There are two major advantages to using Wal-Mart's online photo-development process. First, the price is certainly right—at about 24 cents per 4×6" print. Second, the Wal-Mart Photo Center is closely tied to real-world Wal-Mart stores. You can eliminate the shipping and handling charge on your prints by uploading the images to Wal-Mart's Web site and picking them up at a Wal-Mart store one hour later. You also can have your nondigital camera prints added to your online photo album if you drop off your film at a Wal-Mart store.

WINKFLASH (www.winkflash.com)

At about 16 cents per 4×6" print, Winkflash is one of the most inexpensive online photo developers we've found, making it especially appealing to those who need to catch up on their growing stash of digital photos.

But the appeal doesn't stop there. Winkflash also gets high marks for quality and its wide range of print sizes. Many online reviewers praised it for its simplicity of use and its fidelity to the original print quality. Winkflash's high-quality photos paired with its flat shipping fee of 99 cents per photo order (no matter the quantity of photos) makes it a wise economical choice.

In addition, unlimited online storage space makes it convenient for friends and family to view and order photos online.

SNAPFISH features more than 20 kinds of gifts you can make with your snapshots.

SNAPFISH (www.snapfish.com)

In terms of price, Snapfish falls in the midrange of online developing services, with 4×6" prints starting at about 19 cents apiece. It's not unlike some other services, allowing you to easily upload pictures and enhance them with customized borders and effects.

Where Snapfish shines, though, is with the sheer volume of ways in which you can print your pictures on things besides paper. In the gifts section, you can choose to have your image emblazoned on calendars, sweatshirts, mouse pads, scarves, puzzles, pet bowls, playing cards, plates, holiday ornaments—and that's only about half of

your options. Some of them are pricey (a necktie with your favorite picture on it will set you back $24.99), but they're definitely creative.

Many of these online photo developers offer introductory specials, such as free prints or reduced shipping charges, in order to get you hooked on their service. And most offer an uploading option and a mail-in option for getting your images to them.

Our advice: Shop around for a deal and take advantage of it for a picture or two. Once you find a service that offers the quality and features you like, that old ink-jet printer may find new life as a doorstop.

More to Explore

Here are links to a few of the dozens of online photo developers. Additionally, your local photo processor may offer digital prints at competitive prices, so be sure to look around for bargains.

36pix – www.36pix.com
Club Photo – www.clubphoto.com
dotPhoto – www.dotphoto.com
ezprints – www.ezprints.com
ImageStation – www.imagestation.com
Ofoto – www.ofoto.com
PhotoWorks – www.photoworks.com

software **solutions**

COMPUTER SCRAPBOOKING SOFTWARE CAN MAKE DESIGNING LAYOUTS DIGITALLY A SNAP.

ARTICLE BY PATRICK SOLOMON

THE PHOTO-SYSTEMS MANIPULATION TOOLS in My Scrapbook 2 software by Ulead are outstanding, offering many advanced features at an attractive entry-level price.

the computer

isn't likely to replace scissors and glue sticks in the scrapbooker's arsenal. Thumbing through an album elicits a more emotional response than clicking through Web pages or flipping through a stapled packet of pages from your ink-jet printer. But "virtual scrapbooking" has its advantages. You can use your computer to try out designs before making that first cut. You can easily print out formatted text or clip art to add to your real scrapbook. And you can share perfect copies of your virtual scrapbooks with many people—something you probably would never be able to do with actual scrapbook pages.

Several software packages can help you create scrapbook elements or complete virtual scrapbooks. Here are brief reviews of some of them. Most can be found at bookstores, scrapbook specialty stores, and software retailers.

ART EXPLOSION SCRAPBOOK FACTORY DELUXE ($39.99, Nova Development). Don't let the name fool you; this software does more than just scrapbooks. It can help you create journals, trading cards, brag books, photo frames, stickers, Web pages, slide shows, family trees, and more. And unlike some Swiss Army Knife packages, this one handles scrapbook duties quite well—if you're a beginner. Select from the more than 2,500 logically sorted templates and follow the on-screen directions. The included array of more than 25,000 clip art graphics and 500 fonts are of very good quality, which, at the price, comes as a happy surprise.

If your photography skills aren't up to snuff, the advanced photo editor can fix red-eye, bring photographs into focus, and repair other problems; conversely, if your digital photos look too good, you can make them look wrinkled or like antique photos (complete with scratches). When you're finished with your digital scrapbook pages, you can easily burn them on CDs, complete with music, and play them on your home DVD player. Scrapbook Factory requires Windows 98 or later, 64 megabytes of RAM, and a Pentium 166 MHz processor or the equivalent.

HALLMARK SCRAPBOOK STUDIO 2 ($19.99, Sierra Home).

Scrapbook Studio 2 claims to do many of the same things as Scrapbook Factory Deluxe, and it's half the price. But along with the price reduction, you get a reduced number of templates, graphics, projects, and fonts. Because the software is from Hallmark, it's easy to add a "Hallmark Phrase" to any project. But the photo-editing tools aren't easy to use. Instead of being integrated into the Scrapbook Studio 2 program, the photo editor is a separate program. Scrapbook Studio 2 requires Windows 95 or later, 32 megabytes of RAM, and a Pentium 200 MHz processor or equivalent.

ULEAD PHOTO EXPRESS MY SCRAPBOOK 2 ($29.95, Ulead Systems).

This amazing software doesn't have nearly as many graphics, templates, and fonts as Scrapbook Factory Deluxe, but it excels at photo organization and manipulation. Tired of looking at all those unrecognizable numbers your camera gives to your photos? You can easily change a series of digital photos into names that finally make sense. Forgot to turn on your flash? The new Fill Flash feature adds highlights to an image for you. Don't like square photos? You can choose from 30 other shapes. Don't know how to color-correct an image? The program gives you many options, letting you select which one looks best.

Some features are similar to ones in photo-manipulation programs that cost hundreds of dollars—and the ones in My Scrapbook 2 are faster and easier to use. Because there are so few templates, though, you might use My Scrapbook 2 to touch up your photos before exporting them to another program. My Scrapbook 2 requires Windows 98 SE or later, 64 megabytes of RAM, and a Pentium III 700 MHz processor or the equivalent.

INDESIGN 2.0 ($699, Adobe Systems) and QUARKXPRESS 5.0 ($899, Quark).

These are powerful programs with powerful prices, but if you're serious about wanting to scrapbook from scratch on your computer, these professional-grade programs can help you create any page you can imagine. Don't expect templates and clever sayings here; what you'll find are tools to manipulate text and photos in nearly any combination, shape, color, and size. On the plus side, you've got absolute control over every element on your page, and you can use either program to create books, flyers, posters, newsletters, or anything else that can be printed. On the downside, there's a fairly steep learning curve to get the best results—but if you become proficient at either program, you've also got a valuable

occupational skill. InDesign requires a Pentium II or G3 processor, Windows 98 or Mac OS 9.1, and 128 megabytes of RAM. QuarkXPress requires a Pentium or Power PC processor, Windows 95 or Mac OS 8.6, and 32 megabytes of RAM.

So, although you may not be tempted to retire your glue sticks any time soon, it's easy to find a computer program that can enhance the look and creativity of your scrapbooks—virtual or otherwise.

finding your roots

WITH THE CLICK OF A MOUSE, YOU CAN EXPLORE YOUR FAMILY'S LINEAGE ON ONLINE GENEALOGY SITES.

ARTICLE BY PATRICK SOLOMON

as far as scrapbooking themes go, genealogy—commonly known as heritage—is among the most popular. Genealogy can be laborious and studious. There are even universities where you can get a degree in it. But you don't have to devote four years of your life to develop a great heritage scrapbook. Unlike previous generations—wherein family research involved poring over dusty tomes and traveling abroad to find documents and interview long-lost relatives—you've got a computer. Here are some Web sites and software that can help you discover more about the people and places that came before you.

THE U.S. NATIONAL ARCHIVES AND RECORDS ADMINISTRATION

(www.archives.gov/research-genealogy) is a great place to start. There are census documents, research guides, forms for requesting information (including military service records, ship passenger arrival lists, and land records dating back more than 200 years), and microfilm catalogs available online. This site isn't the most user-friendly, but the research and how-to guides are worth a look.

WORLD-WIDE GENEALOGY RESOURCES

(www.genhomepage.com/world.html) offers genealogy links that are specific to about half the world's countries. Western countries are better represented than Eastern ones (for example, Sri Lanka has one link while Ireland has 50), but there's a surprising depth to the information available. This isn't just for international research, though; each state in the union has links as well. Although you'll likely run into a broken link or two, you'll still find information for just about anywhere your ancestors called home.

CYNDI'S LIST OF GENEALOGY SITES ON THE INTERNET

(www.cyndislist.com) has to be seen to be believed. It offers more than 220,000 links to categorized and cross-linked resources you'd be hard-pressed to find any other way. Got an ancestor who served in the Canadian military in New Brunswick? There are five links to get you started. Hit a brick wall during your research? There are dozens of links on how to get back on track. If you can't find a specific category, you can easily search the entire site. And although I haven't clicked on all 220,000 links, every one I have clicked on has worked.

If you already have some research under your belt and you're ready to start compiling information, here's our software picks that may help:

FAMILY TREE MAKER 2005 (www.ftm2005.com) is an excellent way to build and share your family tree. Family Tree Maker has for years simplified the way we build family trees, but this new version for 2005 has made merging information from the Web easier. Use the wizard to accept new data in one step, or choose which specific information you want to incorporate—all without the fear of overwriting your existing information. A new Web Search report also allows you to easily compare information found online with your existing data. You even can add a bookmark in your tree so you can jump to people you view frequently. Family Tree Maker 2005 costs $29.99 and requires Windows 98/ME/XP or later.

ANCESTRAL QUEST 11 (Incline Software, www.ancquest.com) has some intriguing features. After you enter information in the database, you can request a variety of reports and charts (even birthday and anniversary reminder calendars) that you can share with others via PDFs. The program also can

KISSING JOSH

Striving to create a clean, uncomplicated palette for her layout, designer Kayla Schwisow enlarged the photograph of her with her brother, made it black-and-white, and paired it with papers in various shades of red. Kayla used Adobe InDesign to create a journaling block with white text against a pink background. To fashion a heart embellishment at the top of the page, she creatively turned a cursive metal letter "L" on its side.

SOURCES: COMPUTER FONT IS OPPIE'S MA, DOWNLOADED OFF THE INTERNET. METAL LETTER AND METAL-RIM TAGS BY MAKING MEMORIES. **DESIGN BY KAYLA SCHWISOW.**

Having a sister is like having a best friend you can't get rid of. You know whatever you do she'll still be there.

Sept. 2002

BLESSINGS OF GRANDPARENTS

Since becoming a mother, Ali Edwards has admired the dual role her mom and dad play as her parents as well as grandparents to her son, Simon. Knowing this page devoted to her parents would have a lot of journaling, she began by computer-generating her text, leaving room for the stamped accents she added later. To highlight the "parent" aspect of their dual roles, Ali used a bolder typeface every time the word appeared in her layout. She used Adobe Photoshop to print the title on an enlarged photo, mounting it on patterned paper and then stamping a sentence from her journaling below it. She also added metal-rim tags decorated with printed circle cutouts and stamped with additional letters and words.

SOURCES: CARD STOCK BY BAZZILL BASICS PAPER. PATTERNED PAPER AND CIRCLE CUTOUTS BY KI MEMORIES. COMPUTER FONTS ARE ARIAL AND ARIAL BOLD BY MICROSOFT, AND CEZANNE BY P22 ("BLESSING"). RUBBER STAMPS BY HERO ARTS ("THANK YOU" AND LETTERS FOR CAPTIONS) AND PSX ("TIME"). METAL-RIM TAGS BY EK SUCCESS. DESIGN BY ALI EDWARDS.

NATURAL GRANDPARENTS

Jennifer McGuire's parents love their step-granddaughters as if they had a shared ancestry. So, when Grandma and Granddad Ditz took the girls on a full-day adventure, Jennifer used the photos she took as the basis for this layout about their bond.

Although the special photos are worth a thousand words, the journaling reveals Jennifer's gratitude toward her parents. She included plenty of journaling, occasionally using colored ink to highlight key phrases. At the end of the journaling block, she emphasized a few especially important words by increasing the type size and using multiple colors for the phrase. She left extra space on one side of the main photo mat for her title, which is a combination of rubber-stamped words, a matted stencil letter, and alphabet stickers.

SOURCES: CARD STOCK BY BAZZILL BASICS PAPER. PATTERNED PAPER BY KI MEMORIES. FONT IS RED DOG BY TWO PEAS IN A BUCKET. STICKERS BY KI MEMORIES (BLACK LETTERS AND WHITE LETTERS IN BLACK RECTANGLES) AND EK SUCCESS (BLACK LETTERS IN WHITE PRINTED CIRCLES). RUBBER STAMPS BY HERO ARTS. TAG AND STENCIL LETTER BY AUTUMN LEAVES. **DESIGN BY JENNIFER MCGUIRE.**

COLOR ME
HAPPY

Curiosity got the best of Donna Downey's youngest child, Payton. Payton's big sister didn't want to share, so as soon as Big Sister headed off for an afternoon nap, Payton got her hands on the crayons. Mom watched and photographed as Payton inspected each crayon and figured out exactly how they work.

Donna used text-editing software to type her journaling and to change the color of the text. She also left room to add four smaller square photos. For the left page, she used square punches to make small frames from each shade of card stock. After adhering the squares to the page, she simply stamped the letters of the word "color" in the openings.

SOURCES: PUNCHES BY MARVY UCHIDA. RUBBER STAMPS ARE CELTIC CAPS BY PSX. COMPUTER FONT IS GARAMOUCHE BY P22. **DESIGN BY DONNA DOWNEY.**

Color Me Happy...

You would patiently watch your sister as she grabbed fistfuls of crayons from the drawer and carefully arrange them on the drawing table above. Curiously, you would inch yourself closer to watch her as she would use each crayon before deciding on a color. With every inch you gained, McKenna would move that much more over to block you from intruding on her play. If perchance one of her stray crayons would roll to the floor you would scurry to it. Then, just as you were about to reach for the crayon, McKenna's tiny hands would reach down and scoop it up first. She would then follow it up with a resounding, "No crayon Pay-ton!" and the unmistakable finger wave.

However one afternoon while McKenna was taking a nap, I found you sitting on McKenna's step-stool elbow deep in crayons. Amazingly enough you managed to keep yourself steady as you touched each crayon on the table. It was awesome to watch you inspect each crayon as if you were wondering what it was you were really missing all this time. I don't think you were quite sure what you were supposed to do with them at first. Eventually, as you began flailing your arms about and the crayons would leave light brush marks across the paper.

June 2002

PAINT A PONY

Polly Maly ran a transparent sheet through her ink-jet printer to generate a clear journaling overlay for this layout. To emphasize certain words in the song-lyric journaling, she changed the typeface and ink color. She attached the transparency to the background with small eyelets and adhered the title letters on top.

SOURCES: CARD STOCK BY BAZZILL BASICS PAPER. TRANSPARENCY FILM BY 3M. COMPUTER FONTS ARE FIORI ("WATERCOLOR PONIES") BY TWO PEAS IN A BUCKET AND ECHELON (LYRICS), DOWNLOADED OFF THE INTERNET. PEWTER LETTERS BY CREATIVE IMAGINATIONS. EYELETS BY DOODLEBUG DESIGN. WATERCOLOR PAINTS BY REEVES. SONG LYRICS BY WAYNE WATSON. **DESIGN BY POLLY MALY.**

AUTUMN IS A SECOND SPRING

To convey a feeling of warmth and serenity in her layout, Melissa Chapman chose this photo of her daughter, Madisson, playing in a pile of leaves on a warm fall day. She began the simple layout by machine-stitching a rich shade of textured paper to the card stock background on which she'd already printed a seasonal quote. Melissa used additional machine stitching to attach her photo to a card stock mat. Her title, computer-printed on twill tape and clipped to a photo-realistic die cut, is the finishing touch.

SOURCES: CARD STOCK BY BAZZILL BASICS PAPER. TEXTURED PAPER BY SCRAPBOOK SALLY. COMPUTER FONTS ARE COPPERPLATE LIGHT ("FLOWER") BY URW++ AND TEXAS HERO (TITLE) BY AGFA MONOTYPE. DIE CUT BY PAPER HOUSE PRODUCTIONS. CLIPS BY AVERY DENNISON. **DESIGN BY MELISSA CHAPMAN.**

ADVANCE TO HAWTHORNE AVE.

For this layout, Tracy Kyle used a panoramic photo snapped as the family headed out for their new home. She mounted the photo near the bottom of the page and then covered the right side of it with a strip of vellum on which the street address was printed. Inspired by the game Monopoly, she used elements reminiscent of the game to design a title and pocket for a journaling tag.

SOURCES: CARD STOCK BY BAZZILL BASICS. PATTERNED VELLUM BY MEMORIES IN THE MAKING FOR LEISURE ARTS. STICKER BY STICKER STUDIO. COMPUTER FONTS ARE ARIAL BY AGFA-MONOTYPE AND MONOPOLYBATS DOWNLOADED OFF THE INTERNET. PEN IS A SLICK WRITER BY AMERICAN CRAFTS. POSTAGE STAMP PUNCH BY EK SUCCESS. RIBBON BY OFFRAY. TAG HOLDER IS TRACY'S DESIGN. PATTERN ON PAGE 93. **DESIGN BY TRACY KYLE.**

YOUR HAND

Amy Grendell tracked important moments during her pregnancy on a monthly calendar that she created in a word-processing program. Here, she paired the calendar page with an ultrasound image of her baby, choosing patterned papers and playful type to counter the dark printout. To highlight features in the ultrasound and minimize the black background, Amy printed her journaling on a strip of vellum, cut out a window, and laid it over the image.

SOURCES: PATTERNED PAPER AND CUTOUTS BY KI MEMORIES. COMPUTER FONT IS HOT CHOCOLATE BY TWO PEAS IN A BUCKET. ALPHABET STICKERS BY CHATTERBOX. RUBBER STAMPS BY MA VINCI'S RELIQUARY. **DESIGN BY AMY GRENDELL.**

FIRST BASE
BIRTHDAY

When Shannon Tidwell's little slugger Maddox turned one year old, she celebrated by throwing a party with an all-American theme—baseball! Not only were the cake and decorations themed, but the birthday boy himself was decked out in a baseball uniform and cap.

The round, red circles are a bold graphic addition, and they reinforce the baseball theme without being literal replicas. Shannon added dimension by chalking the circle edges as well as the edges of her journaling strips. She made sure the first-birthday theme had a strong presence by reverse-printing and cutting out a giant "1" from blue card stock, using alphabet stamps to spell out "one" on the photo mat, and adding a metal number colored with acrylic paint.

SOURCES: CARD STOCK BY BAZZILL BASICS PAPER. COMPUTER FONT IS JACK FROST BY TWO PEAS IN A BUCKET. RUBBER STAMP BY HERO ARTS. METAL NUMBER BY MAKING MEMORIES. CANDLE STICKERS BY EK SUCCESS. **DESIGN BY SHANNON TIDWELL.**

ATHLETE IN
TRAINING

Every baseball hall-of-famer starts somewhere. Renee Villalobos-Campa's son Michael started his career with determination in his first T-ball game, as shown in these photos.

Renee's baseball journaling block—documenting the big game—was printed twice. After creating and printing the text in 4½" circles, she tore one sheet into three separate sections with curved edges to create the two outside pieces of her final ball. She then matched up the text with the intact circle and hand-stitched the papers together. She also created a belt along the bottom of her page by stitching together strips of patterned paper and looping them through D-rings that make up the belt buckle.

SOURCES: PATTERNED PAPER BY 7GYPSIES. COMPUTER FONT IS ATTIC DOWNLOADED OFF THE INTERNET. STICKERS BY CREATIVE IMAGINATIONS (TITLE AND WORDS ON PHOTOS) AND MAKING MEMORIES (DEFINITIONS). DATE STAMP AND BRADS BY MAKING MEMORIES. STAMP INKS ARE CLEARSNAP AND STAZON BY TSUKINEKO. COLUZZLE CIRCLE TEMPLATE BY PROVO CRAFT. **DESIGN BY RENEE VILLALOBOS-CAMPA.**

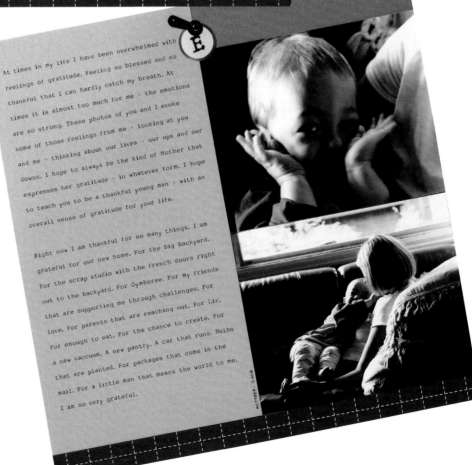

GRATITUDE

Ali Edwards's journaling and creative title treatment complement the striking photographs on these pages by noting the many things for which she is grateful. She created the title in Macromedia Freehand with the dictionary definition of the word "gratitude" framing the title word. A combination of muted-color card stock and strips of design paper create an uncomplicated canvas for her black-and-white photos. Ali used photo turns to secure tags adorned with her son's and her own initials.

SOURCES: CARD STOCK BY BAZZILL BASICS PAPER. PATTERNED PAPER BY KI MEMORIES. COMPUTER FONTS ARE JACK FROST ("GRATITUDE") BY TWO PEAS IN A BUCKET, MY TYPE OF FONT (DEFINITION), AND AMERICAN TYPEWRITER (JOURNALING), BOTH DOWNLOADED OFF THE INTERNET. PHOTO TURNS BY 7GYPSIES. CIRCLE LETTER ACCENTS BY KAREN FOSTER DESIGN. **DESIGN BY ALI EDWARDS.**

LOVE

Robert Indiana's famous artwork "Love" inspired this simple yet striking layout. After finding and downloading a suitable font on the Internet for the title, Heather Melzer computer-printed the letters and then cut them out with a craft knife. She mounted the letters to a sheet of card stock for the background, and then laid vellum over the letters to subdue them before mounting the piece on a slightly larger sheet of black card stock. Before placing the matted photo in the center of the page, Heather wrapped the piece with pink gingham ribbon and mounted it on pink card stock.

SOURCES: CARD STOCK BY BAZZILL BASICS PAPER. COMPUTER FONT IS ANTIQUE TYPE, DOWNLOADED OFF THE INTERNET. LETTERING PATTERN ON PAGE 93. **DESIGN BY HEATHER MELZER.**

better saved than sorry

IT NEVER HURTS TO BE A COPYCAT. MAKE DIGITAL SCANS OF YOUR SCRAPBOOK PAGES AND PHOTOGRAPHS TO PROTECT YOUR TREASURED CREATIONS.

ARTICLE BY PATRICK SOLOMON

fortunately for most of us, it's a hypothetical question: If your house were on fire and your family already safe, what would you try to save?

Your answer probably would have something to do with your photographs or scrapbooks. But feel free to come up with a different answer, because I have a suggestion to help you protect your priceless photos and scrapbooks: Digitize them and store the disks off-site.

Quality digital scans of your irreplaceable prints, negatives, and scrapbook pages can be stored on CD or DVD media and used to create new paper copies should something happen to the originals. Disks also can be copied and distributed among family and friends, providing you with multiple backups and a way of sharing the fruits of your scrapbooking labors.

You can make digital copies yourself with only basic equipment. If you lack the equipment and technical prowess, hire a professional to do the job.

DO IT YOURSELF

If you already have a scanner and a DVD or CD burner, you're well on your way to saving your photographs and pages. If you work with 8½×11" pages or smaller, your standard flatbed scanner should work fine if you can close the lid on the page and any embellishments. Most in-home scanners can't accommodate 12×12" pages or spreads. For oversize pages, Adobe Photoshop Elements has an automatic stitching feature that allows you to scan portions of large pages and invisibly "stitch" them together.

For best results with photo negatives, use a film scanner and scan at the highest quality setting on a clean scanner. Using a transparency adapter on a flatbed scanner to scan negatives at the highest quality setting is the second most desirable choice. Although you can scan printed photographs on a flatbed scanner at the highest quality setting, the results will be less accurate. For fragile heritage photographs, scanning is one sure way to preserve them and, with photo-editing software, even improve their appearance.

Remember to save your scanned images in a format that degrades very little, such as TIFF. Although JPEG files are smaller—which allows you to store more of them on a CD or DVD—they're also of a lower quality.

PROFESSIONAL SCANNING

Have your photos and scrapbook pages professionally scanned if you lack the proper equipment or have particularly large or bulky pages. Businesses that specialize in document scanning (look under "Scanning Services" in the Yellow Pages) can convert your existing layouts into digital images. For double pages that you'd like to view as a single image, tell the scanning service that you want facing pages.

One professional scanning Web site, Twin Imaging Technology, says it can scan "lumpy" pages. I was curious to find out just how lumpy they could be. Owner Gina Martin says, "We have a huge scanner—14×17". The lid can expand up to 2" high. I've never had to go much beyond about ½" thick, even for pages with a lot of hidden journaling." If a scrapbook layout has elements that reach more than 2" high, Martin says she would use a digital camera to take a snapshot of it for posterity. "You won't have all the texture, but you'll have the look [with the photo]," she says.

For snapshots only, many photo labs offer scanning services. They can place your scans on CDs or DVDs in a variety of digital formats, so be sure to specify archival quality.

Professional scanning equipment will capture a higher-quality image than in-home scanners, and the professionals

WHETHER YOU DECIDE TO DO YOUR OWN SCANNING OR SEND YOUR PHOTOS OUT, MAKE SURE YOU KEEP A SET OF YOUR DIGITAL ARCHIVES SOME- WHERE OTHER THAN IN YOUR HOME.

usually can correct flaws (such as dust, scratches, and tears) in photographs. But these services can be expensive, especially if your images need a lot of retouching. Prices vary widely, so try to get at least two bids on your project before you commit.

Whether you decide to do your own scanning or send your photos out, make sure you keep a set of your digital archives somewhere other than in your home. Send a duplicate to a relative or friend who can enjoy the images and keep the disk in a safe place. To be on the safe side, archivists recommend that you make and check copies of your CDs or DVDs once a year to avoid data loss that can result from scratches or age. For optimal care, make certain to store your disks at room temperature and away from light, heat, cold, dry air, and moisture.

Follow these bits of advice and the next time someone asks you that hypothetical fire question, choose to save your china instead, knowing that your photographs and scrapbooks live on in digital perfection.

Long-Distance Options

If you're unable to find local scanning services, here are some long-distance options:

TWIN IMAGING TECHNOLOGY (www.twinimaging.com), located in Carlsbad, California, can accommodate pages that are up to 2" thick.

U DESIGN IMAGE WORKS (www.udesignimageworks.com), located in Orlando, offers photo restoration and archival services. The company uses archival-quality CDs that last longer than the 50-pack variety sold at computer superstores. You'll also receive a printed copy of the scanned documents for reference.

THAT SCRAPBOOK LADY (www.thatscrapbooklady.com), located in Virginia, Illinois, offers high-resolution scans of full scrapbook layouts. If anything ever happens to the original pages, you can send the digital copy back and the company will print a copy using archival-quality paper and ink.

digital
photo magic

USE YOUR IMAGE-EDITING SOFTWARE
AND A FEW SIMPLE TRICKS TO TURN
SO-SO IMAGES INTO STUNNERS.

ARTICLE AND PHOTOS BY ANITA MATEJKA

NOT EVERY PHOTO WE TAKE IS GREAT. TRICKY LIGHTING SITUATIONS, UNAVOIDABLE BACKGROUND ELEMENTS, AND CAMERA FLASH CAN THWART OUR BEST INTENTIONS. THANKFULLY, IN THE DIGITAL-IMAGING WORLD, WE CAN CORRECT THESE PROBLEMS AND ADD CREATIVE TOUCHES TO PUT PIZZAZZ INTO OUR LAYOUTS AND OTHER PROJECTS.

Digital photography is much more forgiving than film photography. You can use digital imaging to improve your photos even without a digital camera. Scan your traditional photos or negatives, save them on your computer, and use photo-editing programs to improve the quality of your pictures. (These instructions refer to Adobe Photoshop Elements and the tools within Photoshop, but most photo-editing programs have similar features.) No matter what my editing goal, I always:

■ **SAVE A COPY** of the photo before beginning to work on it, so I never work on my original image.

■ **MAKE A DUPLICATE** layer of the image I'm working on. I right-click on the description next to the photo in the Layers box (it usually is labeled Background), and select Duplicate Layer. I then do all my editing on the top layer, so if I've saved my file and later realize I don't like something, I can delete the duplicate layer and start over with the original photo. Then I get to work fixing any problems with my photos or adding special touches.

ADJUSTING EXPOSURE

Unfortunately, the sun can play tricks on a camera's light meter (which reads the light coming in and selects the correct—or incorrect—setting accordingly). This can produce photos that are underexposed, meaning not enough light was entering the camera and the photo is too dark (see *Fig. 1*). When too much light enters the camera, the photo is overexposed, and the result is a very bright, light print with loss of detail (see *Fig. 2*).

These images can suffer a loss of quality with certain types of digital correction. For instance, if you use the Levels or Curves tool when correcting, the poorly exposed image becomes grainy. To get better results, do the following:

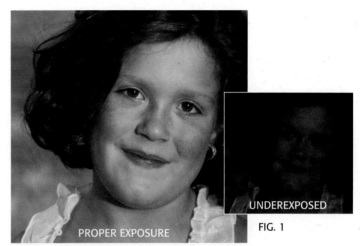

PROPER EXPOSURE

UNDEREXPOSED

FIG. 1

PROPER EXPOSURE

OVEREXPOSED

FIG. 2

1 In Photoshop, a toolbox at the bottom right corner has a tab labeled Layers. Below the tab is a thumbnail of your photo with the label Background next to it. Right-click on Background, and select Duplicate Layer. This creates a duplicate of your photo.

2 Making sure that Duplicate Layer is selected, click on the drop-down menu that is directly below the Layers tab. The default selection is Normal. Change that to Screen. This lightens the image without any resulting noise or grain.

3 If the image is still not light enough, create a duplicate of your top layer (not the background). Since you're duplicating the screened layer, the new layer already will have the screen option selected, and you can lighten it even more. Continue doing this until you're happy with the results.

If your image is overexposed, follow the steps above, but instead of selecting Screen, choose Multiply.

HELPFUL HINT: If the Screen or Multiply layer is too light or dark, change the number in the Opacity box. By clicking on the arrow next to the box, you can adjust the amount and see what works best.

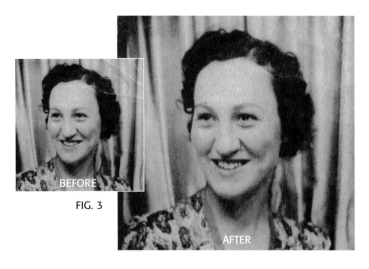

FIG. 3

BEFORE

AFTER

3 If you lose your catch light (the white spot in the pupil from the flash) and want it back, select the Eraser tool, change the brush to the appropriate size, and erase where the spot was. Or create your own catch light by lassoing a small area of the pupil, returning to Hue/Saturation and moving the Lightness slider all the way to the right.

FIG. 4

BEFORE

AFTER

FIXING IMPERFECTIONS

Bent corners, wrinkles, and discoloration often mar cherished heritage photos. But with a little patience and your photo-editing software's clone tool, many of these problems can be fixed easily. The clone tool also removes unwanted elements from any photograph.

The clone tool, generally located on the toolbar on the left side of your computer screen, looks like a stamp with a handle. (When working with the clone tool, save your work frequently; it would be a shame to have to redo this often tedious work.)

Determine the area you will be cloning from. Hold down the Alt key (or the Option key for Mac users) and click on that area. For instance, when working on the photo of my grandmother (Fig. 3), I selected the area directly above or below the white creases in the photo. Keep your brush size small when working in high-detail areas, and work slowly and methodically. You can always use the Undo button (Ctrl + Z) to remove any errors, or click on the History tab to delete several steps. Brush over the area that needs to be fixed. Cloning may take practice, so I suggest starting with a simple task, such as removing a ball from a grassy area. Clone the grassy area and brush over the ball. When working with larger areas, select different areas to clone; otherwise, you may end up with repeating patterns that are too obvious.

Another quick fix for images with distracting clutter is cropping. Removing a problem area in an image can improve the photograph and keep your eye from being distracted. Remember, not all images for your layouts have to be standard image sizes. You can crop and print at any size that your printer allows.

CONQUERING RED-EYE

Many photo-editing programs have a red-eye filter or tool to remove red-eye from your images (see Fig. 4). For best results, I use this simple technique:

1 After creating a duplicate layer, select the lasso tool from the toolbar and set the Feather option to 1 pixel. Carefully lasso the red part of the eye plus about one more pixel.

2 Find the Hue/Saturation selection in the menu bar (under Enhance in Elements), and drag the Lightness slider all the way to the left, which makes the pupil black as it should be.

ADJUSTING COLOR

Fluorescent lighting often results in yellow-tinted images. In Fig. 5, my white balance was set incorrectly, giving the image a green cast. Adjusting color in Elements is as easy as selecting Variations from the Enhance menu. This pulls up your image with a variation of colors, and you can choose which image looks the best.

In Photoshop, use the Color Balance menu option, and move the slider in the opposite direction of the color being removed. For example, the image on the far right was too green, so I slightly slid the button in the opposite direction, which is magenta. Adjust until you find the right color for your image.

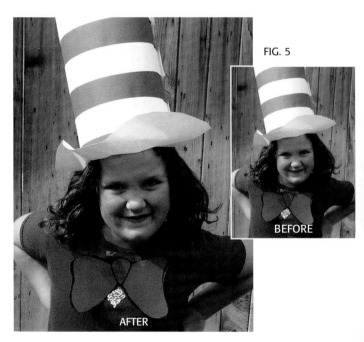

FIG. 5

BEFORE

AFTER

EASY-TO-APPLY BORDERS AND EDGES GIVE PHOTOS A CUSTOM LOOK.

100% PURE JOY. Danelle Johnson wanted to create a soft, feminine layout for this photo of her youngest daughter. She used the brush tool in Adobe Photoshop to soften the image edges and leave a faint watermark in the background. She also included a small file-folder book that contains additional images and journaling.

SOURCES: PATTERNED PAPER BY DESIGN ORIGINALS. STICKERS BY RUSTY PICKLE (VINTAGE CHILDREN) AND ME AND MY BIG IDEAS (FLORAL NAMEPLATE). RUB-ON WORDS BY MAKING MEMORIES (SCRIPT) AND ART WAREHOUSE FOR CREATIVE IMAGINATIONS ("100% PURE JOY"). RUBBER STAMP BY ANNA GRIFFIN FOR ALL NIGHT MEDIA. PHOTO TURNS BY 7GYPSIES. RIVETS BY CHATTERBOX. FILE FOLDERS BY RUSTY PICKLE. RIBBON BY OFFRAY. **DESIGN BY DANELLE JOHNSON.**

I see Him in my *Reflection*

It's taken many years for me to realize what I see in the mirror might be very different from the way others see me. It's fair to say I've never been comfortable with my own reflection. I've always had a difficult time looking at photos of myself. I know many people do. Childhood photos remind me of the physical features that caused my poor self-image.

My parents weren't to blame for the way I felt about myself growing up. They adored me, told me how beautiful I was and loved me completely and unconditionally. Now that I'm a parent, I understand what they saw. I look at Cole and Claire and believe there couldn't be two more beautiful human beings on the face of the earth. Truly, beauty is in the eye of the beholder.

As I mature and grow in my faith, I understand now that God sees me with the same eyes that I see my children. Being dissatisfied with the way He made me is really an insult to my Creator. He deliberately and lovingly planned every part of me for His own purpose and pleasure. I may never consider myself a beauty, but I can be satisfied knowing I am beautiful through His eyes.

REFLECTION. Designer Polly Maly removed the cars cluttering the area behind her head in the image by using the clone tool in Adobe Photoshop Elements and then carefully cropping the shot. She sanded the edges of the images by hand to give them a slightly worn look.

SOURCES: CARD STOCK BY BAZZILL BASICS PAPER. PATTERNED PAPER BY AUTUMN LEAVES. COMPUTER FONT IS MOM'S TYPEWRITER DOWNLOADED OFF THE INTERNET. ALPHABET STICKERS BY TERI MARTIN FOR CREATIVE IMAGINATIONS. RIBBON BY HANNAH SILKS. MIRROR BY THE CARD CONNECTION FOR MICHAELS. EYELETS BY CREATIVE IMAGINATIONS. **DESIGN BY POLLY MALY.**

Sometimes the best option is to transform a photo into a black-and-white image. When the colors in a photo aren't coordinated and they're impossible to work with, change the photo to black-and-white. In Elements, changing an image to black-and-white is a one-step process: Click on the Enhance menu option, select Color, then Remove Color. From there, you might want to add contrast to avoid a flat, dull image.

CREATING SPECIAL EFFECTS

Filters are a fun way to add artistic flair to your layouts. Find a filter that really works with the layout. For instance, in my "Spinning Round" layout, *opposite,* using a motion blur ties in with the feeling of spinning and enhances the theme of the page. Here's how I did it:

1 I started by duplicating the background layer. Then I used the elliptical selection tool with a feather of about 50 and selected the middle portion of the photo.

2 I deleted this portion (on your Layer box, you can see the empty hole in the middle of your image). Then with just the top layer selected, I used the Motion Blur filter. You can select many options within each filter, so take the time to try each one to see what works for your image.

3 Once I achieved the effect I wanted, I merged the two layers before printing the image.

Filters aren't the only tools that can make your photos stand out. Many photo-editing programs come with a plethora of borders you can add to your images. If you're looking for an even larger selection, check programs designed specifically with borders in mind. One of my favorites is the Auto FX Photo/Graphic Edges program with more than 10,000 edges and many ways to customize images.

The number of techniques, filters, and actions available to change the appearance of your photos can make your head spin. Spend some time getting to know your photo-editing program. Open up a photo and play with the different filters that are available with a simple click of the mouse. Mix and match filters by running one filter and then running another one over the first one.

FILTERS ARE A FUN WAY TO ADD ARTISTIC FLAIR TO YOUR LAYOUTS.

SPINNING ROUND. To give the focal-point photo on this layout emphasis and reinforce the theme, Anita used Adobe Photoshop Elements to add a blurred effect to the background. She repeated circular shapes throughout the layout, altering the look of square alphabet stickers using a circle punch. Step-by-step instructions are opposite.

SOURCES: PATTERNED PAPER BY SEI. COMPUTER FONT IS AVALON DOWNLOADED OFF THE INTERNET. ALPHABET STICKERS BY DELUXE DESIGNS. RUB-ON LETTERS AND WORDS BY MAKING MEMORIES ("ROUND") AND LI'L DAVIS DESIGNS (DATE). **DESIGN BY ANITA MATEJKA.**

WATERCOLOR IMAGE. Anita used an Adobe Photoshop filter to get the artistic watercolor look of this image. After making a duplicate layer, she selected the image and applied a paint-daub filter to the entire piece. She added a rough border to the image, printed it on watercolor paper, and tore the edges before framing it.

SOURCES: FRAME BY UMBRA. **DESIGN BY ANITA MATEJKA.**

USE FILTERS TO GIVE IMAGES AN ARTISTIC LOOK AND HIGHLIGHT IMPORTANT DETAILS.

COMBINING IMAGES

Once you feel comfortable with your photo-editing software, try creating a custom photo collage or montage. For help with this technique, I turned to a wonderful reference book, *The Photoshop Book for Digital Photographers* by Scott Kelby, (New Riders Press, 2003). Following Kelby's directions, I created a collage that summed up our trip to Laguna Beach, California, *opposite.* Follow the steps below to make your own collage.

1 Open the image that will appear in the center of your collage, and crop it to the size of your final image.

2 Open the second image, and crop it to be one-third the width of the first image and the same height. Select the cropped image, and copy and paste it into your first selection. This creates a new layer to work with.

3 Move the pasted image to the far right side, and use the Layer Mask button at the bottom of the Layers palette (the button is a circle in the middle of a rectangle). Using the Gradient tool from the toolbox, select the Black to White gradient option, and then select the area you want to fade into the first image. By clicking on one part of your image and dragging out the line, you create an area that will be transparent or masked. Repeat steps 2 and 3 with the third image, add text, and print.

FRESCO FILTER

STAINED GLASS FILTER

DIFFUSED-GLOW FILTER

BEFORE

AFTER

breathtaking views *relaxing* crashing waves

LAGUNA BEACH
2004

amazing dolphins *tidepool discovery* las brisas

LAGUNA BEACH 2004. Anita created a photo montage from three separate images for this layout. By working with different layers, masks, and the gradient tool, she created this fun little "poster" of trip highlights. She added text to the completed collage before printing. Step-by-step instructions are on page 74.

SOURCES: PATTERNED PAPER BY CHATTERBOX (TAN) AND SEI (BLUE HARLEQUIN). COMPUTER FONT IS AVALON DOWNLOADED OFF THE INTERNET. STICKERS BY SONNETS FOR CREATIVE IMAGINATIONS ("CRASHING WAVES" AND "AMAZING DOLPHINS") AND WORDSWORTH ("RELAXING" AND "TIDEPOOL DISCOVERY"). RUB-ON LETTERS BY SCRAPPERWARE FOR CREATIVE IMAGINATIONS ("BREATHTAKING VIEWS" AND "LAS BRISAS"). RIVETS BY CHATTERBOX. **DESIGN BY ANITA MATEJKA.**

WELCOME, LITTLE ONE. Anita used photo-editing software to give the edges of this image a rough look. She printed the image directly on the card stock after adding her message.

SOURCES: COMPUTER FONT IS ANGELINA DOWNLOADED OFF THE INTERNET. CHARM BY WATCH US, INC. PHOTO/GRAPHIC EDGES SOFTWARE BY AUTO FX. **DESIGN BY ANITA MATEJKA.**

BOND OF LOVE. To focus on the close relationship her daughter and mother share, Danelle used a Photoshop filter to spotlight the image of the two sleeping on the couch and leave the unnecessary details in the dark. She created the background for her images by layering patterned paper and a printed transparency.

SOURCES: PATTERNED PAPER BY K&COMPANY. PRINTED TRANSPARENCY BY ART WAREHOUSE FOR CREATIVE IMAGINATIONS. FOAM STAMPS BY MAKING MEMORIES. METAL BOOKPLATE, MINI BOOKLET, TIED COIN, AND PAPER CLIP BY EK SUCCESS. ACRYLIC PAINT BY PLAID. **DESIGN BY DANELLE JOHNSON.**

REMEMBER, NOT ALL IMAGES FOR YOUR LAYOUTS HAVE TO BE STANDARD IMAGE SIZES.

You also can find software specifically designed to automate creating beautiful photo montages. In "Christmas," *opposite*, Mary Larson used Digital Darkroom Photo Editor by Global Star Software to create a photo of the family Christmas tree comprised of other small images of her family. Search online for free or very inexpensive programs that will do the work for you. Simply select the images you want to use and the image that will be the basis for the final product, and the program will create the montage for you.

As you can see, your computer has an abundance of tools right at your fingertips to aid you in transforming your everyday photos into works of art for your scrapbook pages and gifts for friends and family. Start exploring today and see where your creative adventures take you!

CHRISTMAS

...in Arizona means short sleeves, short pants, and cruising on your brand new skates you just got that morning. Grant and Wyatt take full advantage of being native Arizonans.

CHRISTMAS. Mary Larson used image-editing software to create the photo mosaic in this layout. The software is designed to sort through photos on your hard drive or an attached storage device and create a composite from those images by choosing ones with color values that match the original image.

SOURCES: PATTERNED PAPER BY DAISY D'S PAPER CO. COMPUTER FONT IS ESSENTIAL BY TWO PEAS IN A BUCKET. RIBBON AND PHOTO FLIPS BY MAKING MEMORIES. STICKER BY PEBBLES, INC. DIGITAL DARKROOM PHOTO EDITOR SOFTWARE BY GLOBAL STAR SOFTWARE. **DESIGN BY MARY LARSON.**

warh⬤l-inspired

GRAB YOUR DIGITAL PAINT BUCKET, AND TURN A PORTRAIT INTO YOUR OWN POP-ART–INSPIRED CANVAS.

ARTICLE AND PHOTOS BY HELEN NAYLOR

1 Open the picture file you want to edit, create a working copy of the photo using Save As, and select the Photoshop (*.PSD, *.PDD) format.

2 Select the Lasso tool from the Tools window, and remove the photo background by drawing a rough outline around the subject. To select multiple background areas, press Shift (Windows) or Option (Mac) while using the Lasso tool.

3 Making sure that the background is selected, choose Select, Inverse to select the subject, and then Edit, Copy. Create a new document, and make sure the Contents box is set to Transparent. Paste the copied image into the new document, leaving you with a copy of the photo subject on a checkerboard background. Clean the edges of the image using the Eraser tool.

4 Go to Image, Adjustments, and Threshold, and move the triangular slider until the black-and-white version of your subject is clear. You can use the Burn tool to give some areas more contrast. Choose Layer, Duplicate, and name the new layer "Subject."

5 Select the Magic Wand tool, and deselect the Contiguous option in the Options window. Click on a white portion of the subject to select all of the white areas; press Delete on your keyboard. Return to the first layer, and use the Magic Wand tool to click on the background areas of the image. With the background selected, choose Select, Inverse, and then press Delete on your keyboard. Choose the Paint Bucket tool, and click on a deleted area. You should now have a color-filled subject again.

6 Choose Layer, New Layer, and name it "Background." In the Layers window, click on the layer titled Background to select it. Drag the layer to the bottom of the list.

7 Choose Select, All. Choose the Paint Bucket tool; click on any area to fill the background with a different color than the one you used to fill your subject. Experiment with multiple layers and colors to create more intricate color combinations. Save to a new file; you'll use the new file to create several copies of the image for your final art. To make images with other colors, select either Layer 1 or Background, and use the Paint Bucket tool to fill them with different colors.

8 Create a new document for all your altered images. Make the new document size three times wider and taller than your original image. Choose Edit, Paste, and move the image to the top left corner of the new document. Return to the previous window and close it. Do not save the file; you already saved it in Step 7. Choose File, Open, and open the image you saved in Step 7. Make your color adjustments; select the finished image by choosing Layer, Merge Visible, Select, All, Edit, Copy. Return to your new document and choose Edit, Paste. Move this image next to the first.

9 Repeat steps 7 and 8 until the window is filled with different-color versions. Save the document and choose Image, Resize, Image Size. Change the resolution to at least 125 pixels/inch (300 is ideal quality) in the Document Size window and the Resolution box. Change the width and height in the Document Size window to the desired print size. Print.

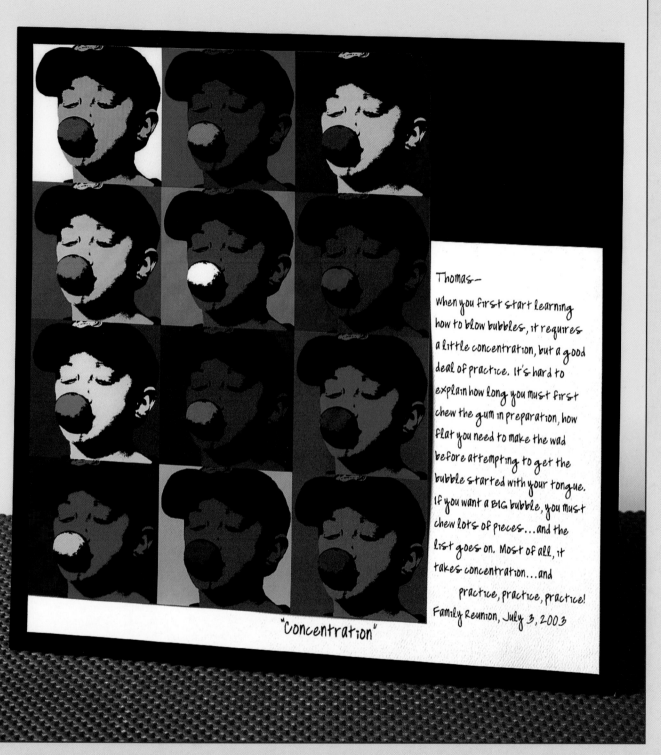

"Concentration"

Thomas—

When you first start learning how to blow bubbles, it requires a little concentration, but a good deal of practice. It's hard to explain how long you must first chew the gum in preparation, how flat you need to make the wad before attempting to get the bubble started with your tongue. If you want a BIG bubble, you must chew lots of pieces...and the list goes on. Most of all, it takes concentration...and

practice, practice, practice!

Family Reunion, July 3, 2003

YOU CAN CREATE your own Warhol-inspired photo montage by using Adobe Photoshop. Select a photo with a clear subject and a well-defined shape for best results.

FROM PLANNING AND PROPPING YOUR PHOTOS TO OVERCOMING THE CHALLENGES OF TRICKY LIGHTING, YOU CAN IMPROVE YOUR PHOTOGRAPHY SKILLS WITH OUR HELPFUL TIPS.

shoot FOR SUCCESS

PHOTOGRAPHER POLLY MALY kept the composition clean in this photo of her two children by simplifying their clothing. Having them both wear white keeps the attention on their faces. Polly also got in close so that their faces filled most of the frame.

a simple plan
Article by Cindy F. Knowles

Whether you shoot your photos digitally or with a traditional film camera, photographs are the heart and soul of most scrapbook pages. They're visual records of our memories, and they tell a story. Without them, no page would be complete. They can make all the difference between a great layout and a so-so one. It only makes sense, then, that we should take the best-looking photos possible to use in our layouts. As daunting as that may seem, taking great photos needn't be confusing or difficult. And although digital cameras have revolutionized the way many of us take photos, the principles of great photography remain the same. By following our six easy steps, you'll find that taking great photos is a snap.

PLAN THE PHOTO SHOOT

Prepare for events you'll be photographing by listing all the elements you might want to record. Consider the main event, as well as preparation, cleanup, and everything in between. Such planning will reduce the chances of missing important shots. Also, think ahead about assembling a scrapbook page. You'll want establishing shots of the group or the location as well as close-ups to provide variety on your layout.

To prepare for taking portraits, collect interesting shots from magazines, catalogs, or advertisements and decide which poses or props you'd like to experiment with in your next photo session.

GATHER SUPPLIES

Stock your camera bag. Keep extra batteries, media cards, or film on hand so you won't miss the unexpected shots—a perfect sunset or your child's funniest face. Plan to shoot more photographs than you expect to use on the scrapbook layout. You also may want to have a portable tripod, lens-cleaning supplies, and a beanbag or two for stabilizing the tripod-mounted camera on uneven surfaces. If you're using film, also keep a pen handy to label the film canister with the date and event immediately after finishing a roll.

When you shoot portraits, collect simple props and set up the backdrop before your subjects are ready. This bit of preparation will make your subjects more comfortable.

USE THE RIGHT PROCESSING AND FILM

If you're using a digital camera, be certain you're setting your camera correctly for the situation. For instance, many digital cameras have an icon of a person running for use in situations when you're photographing quick movement. If you're using film, experiment with different brands and film speeds (ISO ratings). Keep notes listing the results you get with each one on the backs of your photographs, as well as how each functions in indoor and outdoor situations.

Where you have your film developed can make a difference in your finished prints. Try different processing labs until you're pleased with the results. If requested, most photo-processing labs can give your photos a matte finish at no extra charge. A matte finish reduces glare, is easier to work with when hand-fixing red-eye, and doesn't show fingerprints.

Develop a strategy for photo processing based on how you intend to use your photographs. With digital, it's easy to pick and choose exactly which photo you want to print and how many copies you want. With film, some people always order double prints of 4×6" photographs; others order reprints only after they've seen the roll.

STUDY THE LOCATION

Look through the viewfinder to see what the background of your shot will be, and then eliminate any distracting elements, such as objects that might appear to grow out of the heads of your subjects. To reduce background clutter, change the angle of the photograph by standing on a chair and shooting down on your subject, or adjust your camera's aperture so that background elements are out of focus. The smaller the aperture, the greater the depth of field.

Experiment with different types of lighting indoors and out. Shoot photographs at gatherings with and without a flash, and study the results. Even in sunlight, a flash can fill in harsh shadows on faces. And in a dim room, natural light can create an interesting portrait.

USE PROPS TO PUT SUBJECTS AT EASE

When composing a portrait, consider helping your subjects relax by letting them sit or lean on a prop. Props for indoor photo shoots could include an interesting chair, an old suitcase, oversize pillows, or a basket filled with seasonal flowers and plants. It may help your subject strike a more natural pose if she has a prop to hold or something to do with her hands. Great props to use in outdoor photographs include columns, posts, fences, stairs, and arches.

When you include a landmark in a shot, have your subjects stand closer to the camera than the object they're posing by. This technique emphasizes the people but also takes advantage of the landmark as a framing device for the photograph.

POSE PEOPLE

Another way to improve the composition of a photo is to simplify the subject's clothing. Simple lines and solid fabrics, or very small patterns, will help keep the focus on your subject's face.

When photographing a portrait of one person, get in close and don't worry about including all of your subject's body or face. When shooting a group portrait, arrange your subjects in a visual triangle or with each person's eyes at a different level. Another strategy is to compose the group casually by asking your subjects to squish in with their heads together. If you want to see more faces than bodies in the photo, stand above the group and aim the camera down.

Occasionally, despite our best efforts to take a great photo, something goes wrong. Thankfully, it's possible to fix cluttered or blurry photos with today's image-editing software. Image-editing programs also are useful in fixing the dreaded red-eye, as well as adjusting colors. You can compensate for clashing colors by changing the photo to black-and-white or by cropping a photo to eliminate a distracting background.

THESE PHOTOS by Anita Matejka demonstrate the difference made by moving your subject closer to the camera when shooting photos with landmarks in the background. By moving her daughter closer to the camera, she got a great shot while still including the school.

HERE, ANITA DEMONSTRATES how you can put your subjects at ease by using props. In the photo where they're leaning against a tree, the girls look far more relaxed than they do in the shot where they're standing in the open.

in the moment
Article by Erin Terrell

Note the interaction taking place in your favorite family photos. Perhaps you've caught siblings playing together, unaware of the camera. Maybe you've captured a rare kiss on the cheek between grandparents or the look of love between a parent and a newborn child. Whatever the situation, capturing a candid moment between subjects is what most photographers live for. Here are a few guidelines to help you capture a moment of candid interaction:

Be prepared. Have a camera with you (or nearby) at all times. If you're shooting digitally, be sure you have a freshly charged battery and an empty or nearly empty storage card in your camera, and keep extras in your camera bag. If you're shooting with film, keep various speeds on hand to be ready for any lighting situation.

Tell a story. As scrapbookers, we want to tell a story with our photos. The fewer pictures necessary to tell that story, the better. We need to snap more meaningful photos and less of those "strike a pose" shots. That means we're going to have to stop yelling, "Say Cheese!" and instead focus on capturing moments as they naturally occur.

THESE PHOTOS of Erin's daughter and her friend Zac playing outside one summer day illustrate how taking unposed shots of people results in photos that tell the story much better than if the subjects had been posed or looking straight into the camera.

Set the scene. When shooting candid photos, take a cue from photojournalists. Take a few shots to establish the environment and all of the participants. For example, at a wedding or birthday party, you may want one opening shot of the party that includes both the decorations and the attendees.

Reflect relationships. This is more difficult than it sounds. You have to be in just the right place at just the right time to effectively capture on film the relationship between two (or more) people. Position yourself to best capture the moment between your subjects. Watch body language and facial expressions in order to time the moment perfectly.

Remember the details. Once you've captured an interactive shot, you may want to take a few close-up shots to reveal the scene's details. This is where a zoom lens comes in handy. With a telephoto lens, you're able to be unobtrusive and stay far away from the action while still capturing it on film.

If you don't have a telephoto lens or a zoom feature built into your camera, you'll have to zoom the old-fashioned way—with your own two feet. Step in closer to catch the details, but try to remain inconspicuous so you don't ruin the atmosphere.

Keep backgrounds simple. Keeping your background clutter-free will give your photos greater visual impact. Simply switching from one side of your subjects to another may yield a cleaner background. If this isn't possible, try photographing from a higher or lower vantage point. If you know in advance where you'll be photographing your subjects, you may want to remove clutter from the area beforehand.

Another way to diminish a distracting background is to change your aperture to a shallower depth of field. A shallow depth of field will blur background objects and colors and allow less detail to show. It's easiest to blur a background with an SLR camera and a telephoto lens. However, many point-and-shoot cameras feature a "Portrait Mode" setting (the picture of a head on your menu dial) with this option.

With these tips, you should be well on your way to capturing some great memories. The next time you photograph your loved ones, see if you can take some appealing interactive shots.

THE SINGLE-COLOR background of green leaves provides a perfect uncluttered backdrop, which allows the people in this photo to stand out.

ZOOM: This photo of Tracy Kyle's son with his catch of the day illustrates what an impact zooming in and selective focus can make. By getting in close to capture just the fish and her son's head, hands, and shoulders, Tracy filled the frame with the important details and eliminated unnecessary and potentially distracting objects.

simple rules Article by Tracy Kyle

Have you ever thought that your photos would be better if you had a more expensive camera? Well, it's not always the camera that makes the difference. Even if your camera is a 3-megapixel digital point-and-shoot model with limited zoom capabilities, you can take better photos if you keep a few simple tips in mind. Follow our advice, and you just might be able to do without that advanced digital SLR equipped with all the latest doodads.

IT'S ALL IN THE DETAILS

It really is all about the details. When you look through your viewfinder, carefully consider what you're photographing. Ignore the smile and use your critical eye to see what else is happening in the photo. Does your husband have parsley in his teeth? Does your daughter have a tree growing out of her head? Do you really want that pile of dirty laundry in the photo? Take a quick look at the distracting details that could ruin an otherwise good photo.

LET THERE BE LIGHT!

Understanding the effects of light is an important part of photography and can make the difference between a good photo and a great one. Watch where the light is falling on your subject and, if necessary, move to the shade to avoid washed-out photos and squinting eyes. Use your flash, even in situations with sufficient light, to fill in shady spots on your subject.

RULES, RULES, RULES

The rule of thirds is a basic design principle that applies to many things, including photography. Close your eyes and imagine a tic-tac-toe pattern of two vertical lines and two horizontal lines. Imagine this pattern each time you look through your viewfinder, and place your subjects at an intersection of these lines.

UNIQUE PERSPECTIVE

An easy way to add interest to a photo is to try a different viewpoint. Not every photo has to be taken head-on and at eye level. Bend down, get higher, sneak behind your subject … try something different.

ZOOM

Use your zoom to eliminate the unnecessary details from the photo. And don't forget that you also use your feet to get closer to the subject. Try to fill the frame of the photo so you won't need to crop later.

NO MORE POSING

Some of my favorite photos are ones that I've taken while following my children around. Keep your camera handy and ready to shoot photos—you don't want to miss an opportunity when it comes along. And be sure to keep extra empty storage cards handy so you're never caught with a full card.

WHERE'S THAT MANUAL?

Your camera manual contains valuable information. Read it from cover to cover. Look for information on focusing and flash distances and on exactly what all the buttons are for. I've read mine numerous times and carry it in my camera bag for easy reference.

SHOOT AND KEEP SHOOTING

If you currently have the same photos on your storage card as you did last Christmas, you're not taking enough photos! Follow the advice of professional photographers—the more photos you take, the better your chances of getting a great shot. Try to use all of the storage space in one or two sessions, and experiment with various camera functions.

KNOW YOUR LAB

The way you print your photos is an important part of the photography process. Using a good digital photo processor can make a significant difference in the quality of your shots. With an ever increasing number of online and self-serve photo labs, it pays to shop around. Try uploading to various photo lab's Web sites, or use self-serve kiosks at a few different processors; you may be amazed at the difference in quality from one to another. Become a frequent customer and get to know what services they offer and what to ask for when you bring in your film, memory card, or CD full of images.

By following these simple tips, you're sure to end up with better photos. Don't worry if these techniques don't come naturally at first. With a little practice, they'll get easier and become second-nature.

PERSPECTIVE: Adding more interest to a photo can be as simple as changing your viewpoint. Tracy shot this photo from a much higher vantage point, resulting in a photo that's more visually appealing than if she'd shot it at eye level.

NO MORE POSING: In these two photos, Tracy demonstrates how taking candid, unposed shots results in photos that look more natural and tell the story better. She was able to capture the wonder of her son's boyhood exploration, *right,* by photographing him as he was engrossed in examining rocks in a stream. And in the photo of Tracy's mother-in-law and daughter, *above,* their expressions convey the close, loving nature of their relationship.

PATTI TSCHAEN used a fast shutter speed and high-speed film to freeze her daughter mid-stroke during a swim meet.

speed of light Article by Elys Mond

Standing in the icy cold of Park City, Utah, watching the bobsleds scream down the track at 90 miles an hour during the 2002 Olympic Winter Games was a thrill. Capturing those moments on film was a challenge. How could I get a clear shot of the bobsled while conveying a sense of how fast that sled was moving? And how could I avoid ending up with a photo of a big red blur?

You can use several methods to capture a great action shot. "How you take an action picture depends on the effect you want," professional sports photographer Ted Cordingley says. "Sometimes you want to freeze the action. But sometimes you want to convey motion."

Using a fast film and a fast shutter speed can freeze the action as it happens. These are the types of action photos most of us take. And they're wonderful for capturing an astonished expression on a child's face or arms flailing mid-leap.

There also are times when you want to capture the blur of motion, such as a shot of a runner crossing the finish line or a bungee jumper stepping off the platform. This can be done by focusing on the subject but using a slower shutter speed. If you hold very still when taking the photo, the background will stay in focus while the subject is recorded as a motion blur.

Another way to give your photos a sense of movement is to use panning. With panning, the moving subject is in focus and the background becomes a blur. Photographers often use panning when they want to convey a sense of power or speed. To take a great panning shot, you need a camera that you can manually control. This means that, as with other special photo techniques, a point-and-shoot camera probably will not give you the effect you want. A good single-lens reflex (SLR) camera is a better choice. A digital camera on which you can set the focus and shutter speed definitely has advantages. You can see the shot immediately and make adjustments to get the image you want.

The first camera setting to adjust for panning is your shutter speed. A fast shutter speed will freeze the motion and create a crisp picture. But to convey a sense of movement, a little blur often is good. Slow the shutter speed for panning. Experiment with speeds ranging from $\frac{1}{8}$ to $\frac{1}{60}$ of a second.

Next, frame your shot and prefocus. One of the most important things you can do to prepare for a great action shot is to know your subject matter. "Understand what you're taking a photo of to know where to look for the best shot," says Cordingley. He knows that when he shoots a baseball game, he's probably going to see the best action at first base. So he sets up his shot there. "That way, the camera doesn't have to catch up to the action," he says. Find a good location that's an appropriate distance from your subject. Look through the viewfinder to set up your shot, imagining where your subject would look best moving through it. Then manually set your focus for that spot.

Once you're ready to take the shot, plant your feet on stable ground. Face toward to the midpoint of your pan. Aim the camera to the beginning point of the pan. As the subject moves, release the shutter and follow the moving subject with the camera. (Note that when the shutter is open, you won't be able to see through the viewfinder of an SLR camera.) Swing your body around to follow the motion of the subject. Follow through with the pan as you would a golf swing. "You have to follow through," Cordingley says. "Any sudden movements will distort your picture."

Before you take the actual photo, practice the pan. Swing your body through the pan to get a feel for the pace and the direction the subject will be traveling.

To improve your panning shots, write down the camera settings you used so you can see which settings created which shot, Cordingley advises. "Note the film speed, shutter speed, and aperture, and see which combination gets you the look you want. That way, you'll be even more prepared the next time you decide to take a panning shot."

Remember, as with any new photographic technique, you may not get the results you want on your first attempt. But with a bit of practice, you'll end up with images you love.

ANITA MATEJKA used a fast shutter speed to catch her daughter as she slid down an inflatable slide, *above*.

VIVIAN SMITH took this photo, *left*, of her daughter playing soccer, panning so the background would be blurred in the shot.

TO CAPTURE her daughter as a semi-silhouette against the blue water of the aquarium tank, Nicole Gartland took this photo, *above*, with a point-and-shoot camera, keeping the lens at an angle to the glass and disabling the flash.

LORI BERGMANN shot the sea horse in this photo, *left*, with her SLR camera set on the macro setting and no flash, letting her lens touch the glass.

tips & tricks Article by Tracy Kyle

Astounding, surprising, and always awe-inspiring, aquarium sea life and fireworks nearly always have one thing in common—they're a challenge to photograph. Use our helpful tips to overcome low-light conditions and hard-to-capture movement to get photographs you'll be proud of.

AMAZING AQUARIUM SHOTS

An outing to an aquarium lets you get up close and personal with the underwater world. But dim lighting conditions, reflections, and the movement of fish make successful aquarium shots a combination of planning, timing, and luck.

Before you start snapping away, ask about photography restrictions. Many aquariums don't allow flash photography because it disturbs the animals—and the light from your flash would ruin the shot anyway. Disable your flash or cover it with black electrical tape or your hand.

Go toward the light: Choose the aquarium tank with the most light to compensate for not being able to use your flash. Take the photo at a slight angle to the glass tank—anywhere from 20 to 45 degrees—to reduce glare from lights.

Choose the fast-speed option on your point-and-shoot digital camera or use fast-speed film; ISO 400 or 800 works well. Take multiple pictures of the same shot for best results. Have patience: Set up your camera and wait for the fish to swim by you. Watch for places where the fish like to hover, and photograph slow-moving fish close to the glass.

Stability is important in low-light photography. To reduce vibrations and avoid blurry images, use a tripod and cable release, or try to stabilize your camera or body against a solid surface. If possible, use manual focus; auto focus may put the focus on the glass instead of the fish. How close you can get to the aquarium and the fish depends on your camera and lens. Some lenses have a macro setting, allowing you to get within inches of the subject and maintain focus; other lenses require you to stay several feet away. Get as close to the glass as possible, but be careful not to damage your lens.

If you can't get close enough to take pictures of individual fish or a portion of the aquarium, taking photos of the entire tank can be impressive. If you're using an SLR camera, be familiar with how it works and experiment with different manual settings. The amount of light in the room and in the aquarium tank will make each situation a bit different, so try several settings of the same shot for best results.

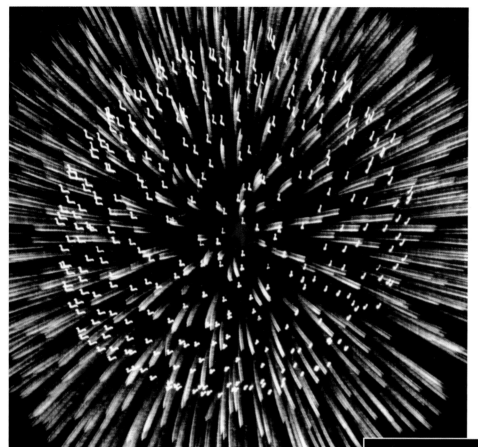

TO CAPTURE the stream of fireworks, *below,* and the word "July" being written by a sparkler, *bottom,* Anita Matejka used a tripod to steady her camera and kept the shutter open for several seconds.

NICOLE GARTLAND'S POINT-AND-SHOOT camera automatically kept the shutter open long enough to capture this photo, *left.* She stabilized her camera by holding her elbows firmly against her body.

FANTASTIC FIREWORKS PHOTOS

Summer evenings bring wonderful opportunities to capture the magic of fireworks in your photos. But taking successful photographs of the stellar light show can be challenging. Here are some hints to help you take great low-light fireworks photos.

Time exposure is key in fireworks photography. As the fireworks rocket through the sky, you'll want your photos to capture both the explosion and the trails of color. To achieve this, you'll need to keep your shutter open from 1 to 20 seconds. By keeping the shutter open so long, you can capture a number of explosions in one photo, which will look spectacular. If using a digital camera, use your nighttime setting for a slower shutter speed. Most digital cameras will adjust automatically and keep the shutter open for the amount of time necessary to get the photo. In most cases, vertical (portrait) photo orientation is preferred for fireworks photos so you can capture their tails and the resulting explosion. If you have a point-and-shoot camera that can't be set for timed exposures, the camera itself might keep the shutter open long enough.

Again, stability is important in low-light situations. To get sharp images with longer exposures, keep your camera perfectly still. This is impossible to do when holding the camera in your hands, so using a tripod is ideal. Or, try propping your camera against a wall, car top, or other solid surface. Often just pressing the shutter button can cause movement; using a cable release is strongly recommended.

Normally, when you're photographing at night, you should use a fast ISO film. But with fireworks photography, use standard film, such as ISO 100 (SLR) or 400 (point-and-shoot).

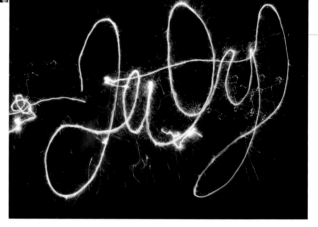

To intensify the fireworks color and keep the sky black, use a small aperture setting such as f/8 or f/11. The right exposure will depend on the speed of film and the brightness of the fireworks; it's a good idea to experiment with different settings. Some higher end digital cameras even have a manual setting that allows you to set the f-stop.

Unless you're trying to photograph a subject in the foreground (such as people or a landmark), you won't need to use your flash. If you can't disable your flash, try covering it with your hand or black electrical tape.

Take lots of shots and have extra film on hand, as the position, color, and beauty of fireworks are unpredictable. Be sure to save some shots for the end—the climaxes usually are spectacular!

patterns

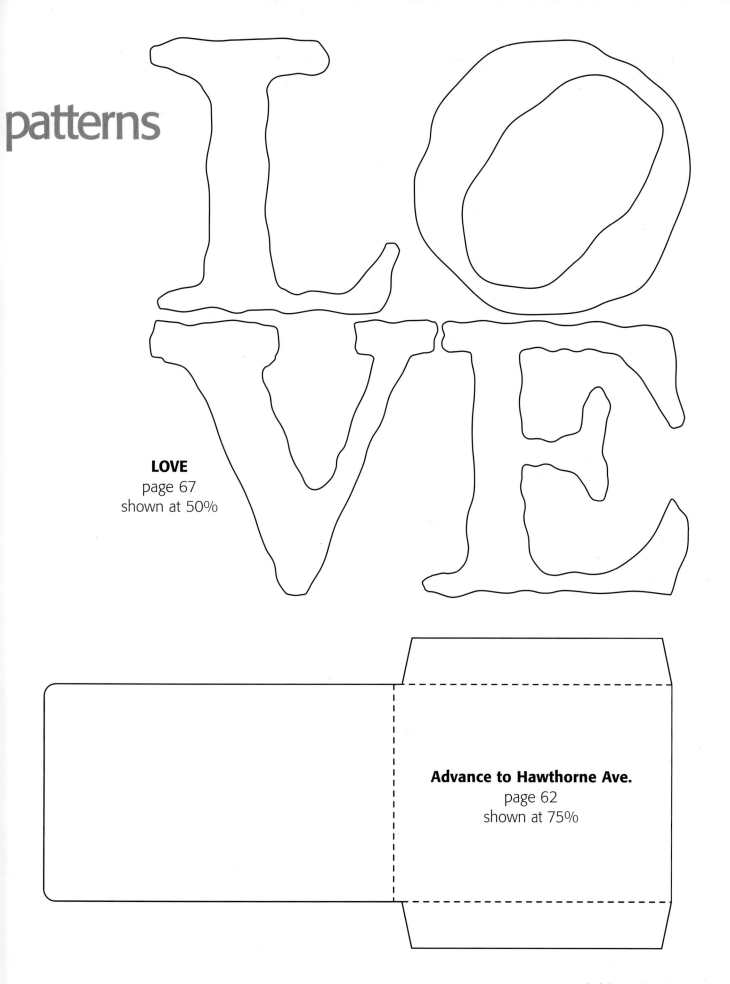

LOVE
page 67
shown at 50%

Advance to Hawthorne Ave.
page 62
shown at 75%

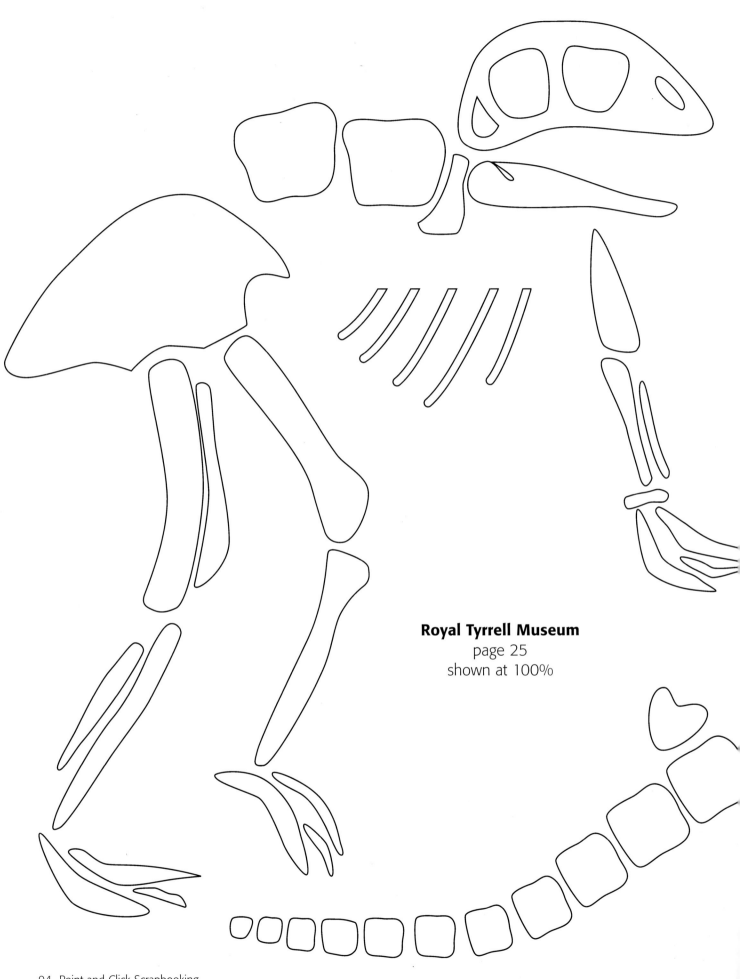

Royal Tyrrell Museum
page 25
shown at 100%

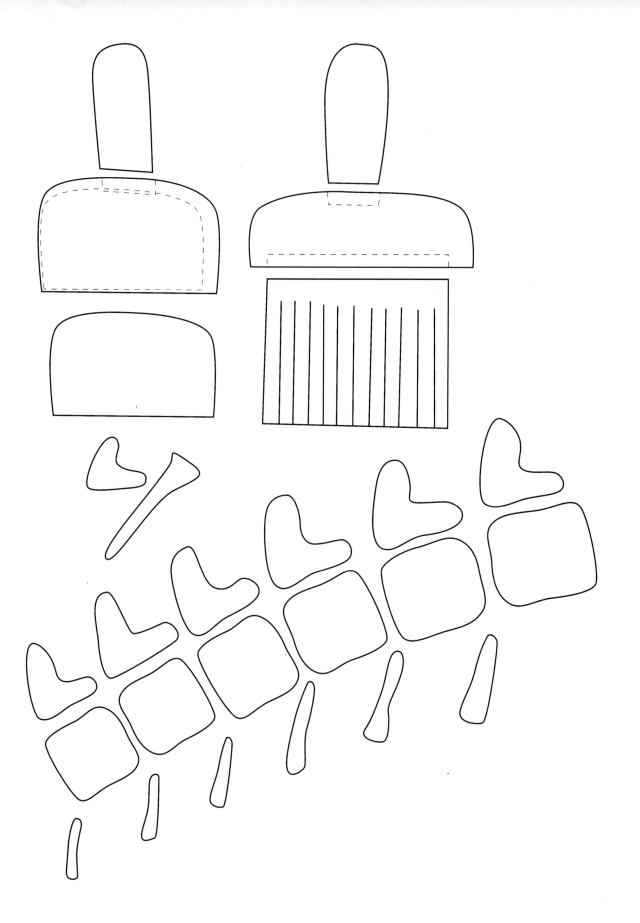

Better Homes and Gardens®
Creative Collection™

Editorial Director
Gayle Goodson Butler

Editor-in-Chief
Beverly Rivers

Executive Editor Karman Wittry Hotchkiss

Art Director	**Editorial Manager**
Brenda Drake Lesch	Ann Blevins

Project Manager	Heidi Palkovic
Contributing Graphic Designer	Tracy S. DeVenney
Copy Chief	Mary Heaton
Contributing Copy Editor	Dave Kirchner
Proofreader	Dana Schmidt
Administrative Assistant	Lori Eggers

Senior Vice President
Bob Mate

Publishing Group President
Jack Griffin

Chairman and CEO	William T. Kerr
President and COO	Stephen M. Lacy

In Memoriam
E. T. Meredith III (1933–2003)